MONOPOLY

STUDIES IN THE BRITISH ECONOMY

General Editor: Derek Lee

Monopoly

by

Derek Lee, *King Edward VI Grammar School, Retford*

Vivian S. Anthony, *King's School, Macclesfield*

and

Allen Skuse, *Haberdashers' Aske's Hatcham Boys' School*

HEINEMANN EDUCATIONAL BOOKS

LONDON

Heinemann Educational Books Ltd
LONDON EDINBURGH MELBOURNE AUCKLAND TORONTO
HONG KONG SINGAPORE KUALA LUMPUR
IBADAN NAIROBI JOHANNESBURG
LUSAKA NEW DELHI

ISBN 0 435 84535 7

First published 1968
Reprinted with corrections 1970
Reprinted 1972
Reprinted with corrections 1975

Published by Heinemann Educational Books Ltd
48 Charles Street, London W1X 8AH
Printed Offset Litho and bound in Great Britain by
Cox & Wyman Ltd, London, Fakenham and Reading

PREFACE

Most Economics text books attempt to cover the subject within a single volume and in consequence some topics are treated briefly: often these same topics are those whose subject matter changes most rapidly. At present in order to keep up to date in the field of economics recourse must be made to a vast field of diffused literature including bank reviews, government publications, newspapers and various journals. With these problems in mind this series was conceived. The series consists of specialized books on those topics which are subject to frequent change or where the sources of information are too scattered to be readily available to the average student. It is intended that each book will be revised at frequent intervals in order to take account of new developments.

The books are written with the needs of Advanced Level candidates especially in mind but they also cover the ground for many professional examinations in economics. The 1975 impression contains a complete revision of facts and figures up to the autumn of 1974.

Derek Lee
Vivian S. Anthony
Allen Skuse

ACKNOWLEDGEMENTS

The following have given permission for questions to be reproduced from their examination papers in economics:

University of London Examination Board
University of Cambridge Local Examinations Syndicate
The Chartered Insurance Institute

CONTENTS

PART 1
THE THEORY OF MONOPOLY

INTRODUCTION

The purpose of this section of the book is to examine the assumptions and conclusions of the simple economic analysis that has been developed to study the behaviour of firms within various industrial structures. This must be done to see what it is about the monopoly situation which sets it apart from other market forms and attracts the attention of the legislator. It is also important to consider all market forms, not only for the sake of this comparison, but also because much 'monopoly legislation' deals, perforce, with situations which are not monopolistic in the strict sense. In theory the monopolist is the sole producer in the market for a certain product. This enables him to behave in particular ways. Such behaviour may, however, also be possible for firms in different market situations. The detailed analysis of each market form is common to most standard textbooks and knowledge of the workings of the various models of the equilibrium of the firm is essential to the reader of this section.[1] For convenience, however, a summary of their assumptions and conclusions is set out below.

1. THE MARKET FORMS

(i) Perfect competition

This market form assumes that there is a large number of small producers; that the good produced by each firm is identical with that produced by its competitors; that there is free entry into and exit from the industry; that there is no collusion between buyers, of whom there should also be a large number, nor between sellers; that both buyers and sellers should have perfect knowledge of the market;

---

[1] We accept at this stage the basic assumption common to models of all market forms: that each entrepreneur tries to maximize his profit. We also work with the simplifying assumption that there exist no stocks, so that total revenue in any time period is equal to the value of current production.

and that there are no transport costs. The result is a model far removed from the real world and one most often considered only as a theoretical limiting case.

It follows that the firm producing under such conditions cannot affect market price. Production is geared to cover costs at this price. This can lead to supernormal profit[1] being received in the short run, but in the long run existing firms will expand and new firms enter the industry until such profits have been competed away. In the final equilibrium position for the firm and the industry each firm is producing at minimum long run average cost which is equal to the price ruling in the market. (This in addition to the basic equilibrium equality of marginal revenue and marginal cost.) Figure 1 shows the familiar short run and long run equilibria positions for the firm in perfect competition.

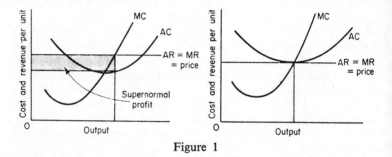

Figure 1

(ii) Monopoly

In contrast the monopolist is assumed to be the sole producer of a particular product which is bought by a large number of people between whom there is no collusion. The permanence of this position results directly from his ability to keep competitors out of his market. Again the assumptions are such as to make this a limiting case. This model, however, does have real world counterparts. The monopolist is found to have control over both price and output, although not independently, and he uses this control to restrict output, raise price, and receive permanent supernormal profits. The equilibrium position is again where marginal revenue is equal to

---

[1] By supernormal profit is meant total revenue minus total opportunity costs, including normal profit, the opportunity cost of capital and risk taking.

marginal cost but in this case price is in excess of these. Figure 2 illustrates the equilibrium position for the monopolist: a permanent position of supernormal profit.

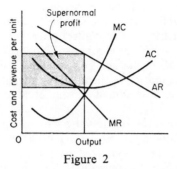

Figure 2

Source of monopoly power – barriers to entry
The power of the monopolist to receive permanent supernormal profits depends on his ability to keep competitors out of his market. There are various ways in which this is done.

In a situation where the market is a large one and the monopolist is therefore producing on a large scale, any economies of large-scale production will ensure that the unit costs of the monopolist will be lower than those of a new and usually small producer. This cost differential alone is enough to keep out competitors. Entry is sometimes forbidden by law, as for example with patents (see second case study). The patent holder has an initial period of time when no competition is allowed. It is likely that subsequently the fact that the patent holder has an established market is sufficient deterrent to would-be competitors. Further examples of monopolies established and perpetuated by law are public utilities, where duplication of service would be inefficient, and nationalized industries. However, since there is the likelihood that in some cases government controlled monopolies will have motives other than profit maximization, one cannot conclude that such bodies necessarily endeavour to make supernormal profits, even where this is possible. One other way in which the monopolist can restrict entry is by direct misuse of the power of his established position. He can threaten supplying firms, arguing that if they supply his new competitor they will lose their established and necessarily larger outlet. He can engage in a price

3

war, which with larger financial reserves, he must win. He can threaten force or engage in industrial sabotage.

Price discrimination[1]

One of the essential differences between perfect competition and monopoly is the ability of the monopolist to control price by varying his output. If, further, he can control price to individual buyers or groups of buyers, and there is no possibility of transfer between the separate sections of the market, he can increase his profits by charging different prices to each of them, taking advantage of the peculiar conditions within each section of the market. Markets can be separated in various ways.

Different geographical location gives rise to automatic separation, especially internationally. The selling of a product very cheaply abroad while a high price is charged in a protected home market is an obvious case of price discrimination. It is of course likely that the producers of the importing country will pressure for a protective import barrier of their own to counteract such 'dumping'. Separation can be achieved over time. The standard example is that of the publishing house which initially offers for sale a hard-back edition of a particular book at a price considerably in excess of that of the paperback edition which follows at a later date. The nature of the product is sometimes enough in itself to establish separation within a market. Heavy equipment forming part of integrated plant and requiring installation by the supplier is not easily resold. More especially, however, is this true of services; it is, for example, impossible to resell medical treatment. Price discrimination is also successful in taking advantage of the fact that some consumers automatically associate a higher price with better quality and are thus willing to pay more for a good if, for example, it is more expensively packaged. The same good can be sold at different prices since the consumers have divided the market themselves.

(iii) Monopolistic or imperfect competition

The monopolistic competitor is one of a large number of producers in an industry into and from which there is free entry and exit. There must be a large number of consumers between whom there is no collusion and they must be faced by an industry which produces a

---

[1] The reader should be able to see price discrimination as a means of eating into consumers' surplus.

large number of similar, but in some way differentiated products. The essential feature of monopolistic competition as compared with perfect competition is seen to be that of product differentiation. The consumer is convinced that differences exist between the various products of the industry. There may be real differences, but it is also possible for each producer to further differentiate in the minds of the consumers by giving the product a brand name, developing a 'brand image' and consequently eliciting a degree of brand loyalty.

It follows from this that the monopolistic competitor has a downward sloping average revenue curve, which produces a short run equilibrium position similar to that of the monopolist. In the short run supernormal profits are received, but in the long run, since there are no barriers to entry, the industry expands and these are competed away. The long run situation is illustrated in Figure 3.

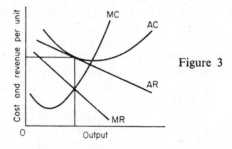

Figure 3

Excess capacity
Again there is a gap between price and marginal cost and, as is shown, the final equilibrium position is one of production at less than optimum capacity; equilibrium is at an output less than that associated with minimum average cost. Each firm therefore has unused or excess capacity and it follows from this that the total production of the industry could be achieved with fewer firms.

Advertising
Product differentiation results from deliberate action on the part of the individual producer, who develops existing, and contrives non-existing, differences between his product and the rest. He does this because it reduces transference away from his product resulting from an increase in his price, and also protects him from similar policies or price decreases by his competitors. Competitive selling, mainly advertising, is thus a feature of this market form. A successful

campaign can, of course, more positively increase short run super-normal profits if consumers are convinced as to the benefit to be gained from transferring brand.

(iv) Oligopoly

The assumptions of oligopoly are less rigid than those of other market forms. There are a few sellers only, each with a sizeable proportion of the market. The product is often differentiated, but sometimes not. Barriers to entry do not necessarily exist although they might be developed in some circumstances. As usual there is assumed to be a large number of consumers between whom there is no collusion. The size of his market relative to that of the industry ensures that the oligopolist also has a degree of control over his price output policy. But the distinguishing feature of this market form is that he has few enough competitors to have to take into account what he thinks their reaction to any decision of his will be. Their actual reaction, whether correctly predicted or not, will of course have a considerable effect on the final result of any decision he does make.

To develop a theory incorporating the numerous variations of reaction and counter-reaction possible in this situation has so far been beyond the economist. The oldest model, due to Cournot and published in 1838, considers two producers only (duopoly) each with zero costs and assumes that neither will react to the other's price-output policy. An equilibrium position is established with the duopolists sharing the market equally between them. It is not easy to generalize from this to the more usual oligopolistic situation. It is in any event of questionable value since the assumptions of zero costs and, particularly, indifference to competitors' policy are hardly realistic. Contemporary economists are endeavouring to develop the Theory of Games, which is the study of behaviour and strategy in the small group situation, and it is likely that a theory will emerge as a result of this. In the absence of the analysis necessary for this study one must simply consider the tendencies in behaviour suggested by empirical study.

Joint profit maximization

The fact that there are but a few firms in an industry facilitates the pursuit of a mutual policy towards monopoly profit. The industry can act as one unit with each firm receiving its share of the maximized profit of the industry as a whole (see first case study). Alternatively the individual firm, by changing its price-output policy, might be able to increase its share of total profit, although this total profit will be reduced as the industry adjusts to this initial move necessarily away from the joint profit maximizing position.

Agreement towards a policy of joint profit maximization is easier the smaller the number of firms, the more homogeneous the product, and the more alike the firms are in structure. In fact where there is no product differentiation at all there can only be one price; if one firm cuts its price all firms must similarly cut theirs or lose their market completely. A mutual price policy is thus inherent in the structure of what is sometimes called 'Perfect Oligopoly'. Collusion will often take place to ensure that price is not competed to too low a level. This most often takes the form of price leadership by the largest producer.

The greatest incentive to break a joint profit maximizing agreement is the fact that the first producer to lower price or further differentiate his product by advertised non-price competition initially gains an increase in his share of the market. Moreover he retains a proportion of this increased share when other firms react with similar policies and the market again settles down.

Restrictive trade practices

The policy of joint profit maximization, involves specific action on the part of the producers in the industry to limit competition and secure the monopolist's prerogative of long run supernormal profits. Deliberate action to restrict competition in any market situation takes many forms (see case studies) and comes under the general heading of Restrictive Trade Practices.

Barriers to entry

If conditions are such that a common policy of joint profit maximization is followed, the supernormal profits consequently enjoyed by the industry can only be a permanent feature if, as with the monopolist, there are barriers to entry. Even where there is no such mutual approach the various barriers outlined below will act to keep new firms out of the industry, to the obvious advantage of established firms.

Where economies of scale exist the individual firm may be large enough to ensure lower unit costs than the necessarily small new entrant, and this cost differential will be barrier enough (see third case study). Where there are no such technological barriers, however, it is still possible to restrict entry. One way to do this is to restrict the share of the market the new producer can achieve by increasing the number of similar but differentiated products made by each firm. Despite brand loyalty a certain proportion of consumers will change their brand at random (not as the result of advertising) in any time period. If there are initially five firms each producing one product, then the new firm can expect to acquire one sixth of the custom of those who change brand in this way. If each firm produces five different brands, then the new firm can only expect to acquire one twenty-sixth of this section of the market; it is probably not worth while.

To maintain its share of the market the individual firm must adversite its brands to at least the same extent as its rivals. Inherent in the development of such advertising is a barrier to entry, for while any increase in selling costs of this kind is unlikely to change the relative market shares of firms within the industry, any new firm must engage in a similar amount of advertising which it can only spread over a necessarily smaller output. The consequent unit cost differential is again probably enough to deter entry to the industry.

Excess capacity

One way in which the oligopolist defends himself against his competitors is to ensure that, unless there is a policy of mutual exclusion, he has similar outlets to those of his rivals. Thus a suburban high street will contain a branch of each of the main joint stock banks, although it is likely that the service provided could be achieved with less of them. It follows that each branch is probably working at less than full capacity. There is thus the possibility of excess capacity in this market form, and where this occurs is again a situation of wastage of resources.

Resale price maintenance

One aspect of product differentiation in both oligopoly and monopolistic competition is the maintenance of a uniform price for a branded good in each retail outlet. The manufacturer argues that the price of his good is part of the brand image, the consumer is likely to consider price as a measure of value or quality, so that any cut in price is detrimental to the brand image, and of course to the manufacturer, as the consumer substitutes away from what he considers to be a poorer quality good. A further motive for such a policy is that it enables the manufacturer to have a large number of retail outlets for his good since the less efficient firms are not forced out of the industry by price competition. Resale price maintenance has therefore been a further contributory factor to the existence of excess capacity in retailing.

The manufacturer retains his control over price by the use of a 'Stop-List'. He cuts off supplies to the deviant retailer who lowers the price of his good. He is of course in a stronger position if other manufacturers will also stop supplies to any retailer who has cut the price of this one good. Such collective action obviously involves reciprocal arrangements.

2. THE ECONOMIC MODEL

Before examining the features and conclusions of each market form outlined in the previous section, it is important to look at the function of the economic model and its limitations. Any economic model will develop within the framework of a set of assumptions. Most of these are made to reduce the complexities of the real world to manageable form; such simplification makes the analysis possible. The conclusions of the model are subsequently qualified to take account of real world complications and, provided such an adjustment is possible and is made, one is justified in using the conclusions in this final form. Some assumptions are, however, more than simplifications. They are basic conditions of the model which, if found not to coincide with real world behaviour, invalidate the model and any conclusions based on it. An example of such an assumption occurs in the various models of the equilibrium of the firm; the assumption of profit maximization. Here are some of the points which have been made as economists have sought to decide whether the assumption is acceptable or not.

It is sometimes argued that since businessmen have no knowledge of such concepts as marginal revenue and marginal cost, it is impossible for them to maximize profits. This is an obvious *non sequitur*. If the businessman (by whatever means) tries to maximize his profits, the economist taking this as the basis of his argument and using his own theoretical tools can predict equilibria positions in various circumstances. The theoretical concepts used are, of course, not meant to be a description of the actual behaviour of the businessman arriving at those positions by his own methods.

There are, however, economists who question the concept of profit maximization itself. Based on empirical evidence of the way businessmen say they behave, economists have developed the hypothesis of 'full cost' pricing. This states that businessmen consider their total costs per unit and then add a mark-up based on their assessment of the market conditions. This mark-up, which is usually a standard percentage of full costs per unit, most probably includes opportunity costs of capital and risk-taking not incorporated by the firm's accountant in the full costs. Equilibrium output is then determined by how much the market will absorb at this price. This is not, however, necessarily at variance with profit maximization, for it can be argued that the traditional mark-up is itself a function of the desire to maximize profit. The fact that mark-ups tend not to stay constant over time supports this view.

Two other suggestions do give alternative motives for business behaviour. The first says that firms aim for a certain rate of profit and that having achieved this they are not concerned particularly with making any more. The second argues that since in many cases there is no entrepreneur as such, that ownership is divorced from control, the managers will tend to maximize sales rather than profits since it is the size of the undertaking on which their status, and salaries, depend. This is part of the organization theory approach which argues that decisions must in any case vary with the structure of management. The large organization for example is often bureaucratic and decision-taking is thus the result of a formalized compromise of differing interests. Decisions are likely to be relatively less progressive and less flexible in such circumstances. Obviously conclusions based on these sort of assumptions will not coincide with those of a theory based on the maximization of short-run profit. There are, however, more points of contact if long-run profit maximization is considered.

A firm could be content to accept less than maximum profit for several reasons. It might feel that such a policy would enable it to retain goodwill, or avoid the attention of 'the authorities', or, finally, to attract fewer competitors. In each case the long-run position would be protected at the expense of losing some short-run profit. The maximization of current sales could lead to the growth that is necessary to maximize long-run profits. The retention of an established price could be due to a time lapse in decision-taking as a result of bureaucratic organization, in which case the situation could be adjusted in the long run. Alternatively it could be a further attempt to retain goodwill, especially if the short-run decision would be to raise price. Again the firm would be taking the long-run view.

Enough has been said to show that the simple assumption of short-run profit maximization does not cover all situations. In some cases it may be possible to incorporate behaviour differences by extension to an assumption of long-run profit maximization. Care must be taken, however, to ensure that this is not just the contrivance of a tidy mind.

In fact no alternative theories to those based on profit maximization have been fully developed. One is forced, therefore, to use theory based on this basic assumption in order to assess the relative merits and demerits of the various market forms from a theoretical standpoint. In doing this one must recognize the need to qualify simple conclusions as the real world situation demands. In particular it must be remembered that for oligopoly, in which market form most manufactured goods are produced, there is no real *theory* of behaviour at all.

3. CONCLUSIONS

As was indicated in the introduction, the legislator is not only interested in monopoly in the strict theoretical sense (what is sometimes called 'unitary monopoly'). It was not until the 1948 Act that a definition of monopoly was formulated for legislative purposes (see Part 2), and then it took as its basis market dominance in classifying as a monopoly any firm which held at least one-third of the market for a particular product. Further legislation was to deal with restrictive practices. In all this the basis for any judgement was to be whether action by firms could be considered 'against the public interest'. This is not an easy thing to define (see below). There is the added complication that what might be in the public interest at one time need not be so at another. An illustration of this is the change which took place in government attitude after the Second World War as the state of trade generally was no longer depressed as in the thirties (see Part 2).

The purpose of this section therefore becomes less one of comparison between market forms, than one of looking for those aspects of any market form which the government considers to be against the public good. If one decides that unitary monopoly is in some way bad, then so is action on the part of oligopolists in acting as a monopoly. Those restrictive practices considered harmful by the government will be included wherever they occur. While discussing each market form one must also indicate other features which could be considered detrimental but against which the government has as yet not introduced legislation or has only followed a policy involving token or experimental measures. Before doing this, however, it is worth

11

examining in detail a comparison which has often been made; that of monopoly as compared with perfect competition.

(i) Monopoly, perfect competition and the allocation of resources

There had for a long time been the feeling that monopoly was wrong and competition right before Adam Smith and other classical economists argued for competition as the best method of resource allocation, and against monopoly inherent in which is the concentration of economic power in the hands of a few. The economic historian will recall that such quasi-monopolistic practices as 'forestalling', 'regrating' and 'engrossing' were condemned in mediaeval times in that the exploitation of temporary scarcity was against the idea of the 'just price'.

The classical argument maintains that if a perfectly competitive industry is monopolized and costs are unaffected, the result will be a contraction of output and a consequently higher selling price. One can show that this does in fact follow from the models used above. Under perfect competition the supply curve of the industry is the sum of the individual firms' marginal cost curves. This is represented by the curve S_{pc} in Figure 4. Where this cuts the demand curve will be the equilibrium position for the industry, with each firm producing where marginal cost equals market price. If the industry is monopolized and costs are unaffected, the industry supply curve is now the monopolist's marginal cost curve, (MC), and he is in equilibrium

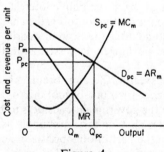

Figure 4

It is demonstrated that more is produced at a lower price under perfect competition than when the industry is monopolized, provided costs remain unchanged.

where this marginal cost equals his marginal revenue, obtained from the demand curve for the industry – now his average revenue curve. As the figure shows, it follows that price is higher and output lower in this situation.

As far as resource allocation is concerned, the argument continues that under perfect competition price equals marginal cost, whereas in the monopoly situation price is in excess of marginal cost. It follows that in perfect competition consumers are allowed to press their demand to the point where further increase in output involves greater cost than revenue, whereas the monopolist prevents such increase in output, even though consumers are prepared to pay more than the cost of such extra production, because he restricts the quantity produced in order to receive supernormal profits. Perfect competition therefore leads to the optimum allocation of resources as determined by the consumer. Wherever there is a gap between price and marginal cost the consumer is being thwarted in his attempt to get what he wants. Thus under perfect competition market forces, Adam Smith's 'invisible hand', automatically give rise to the best allocation of resources.

An extension of the argument – the role of the State
Some economists have extended this conclusion to argue that the greater the degree of competition in any market form, the better the resource allocation. And that any movement away from the freedom of competition, either in the form of market imperfection or intervention by the State, is necessarily bad. But, accepting the proposition as it stands all one knows is that perfect competition gives rise to the best allocation of resources and that wherever price diverges from marginal cost is necessarily a worse position than the comparable perfect competition situation, provided costs are unaltered by market structure. It does not follow from this that a greater *degree* of competition in any market form automatically gives rise to a better allocation of resources. For example, allowing a second gas company to compete in an area already adequately served by an existing company is a positive waste of resources. Further, to approximate more closely to the real world, one must question the assumption of unchanged costs. It is, in fact, very unlikely that if a perfectly competitive industry were monopolized, costs would be unaffected by the change in scale of operations. And it is most likely that unit costs would fall. One can illustrate a case where the reduction in unit costs as the result of the economies of single ownership give rise to greater output and

lower price than the original perfect competition situation. This is done in Figure 5. The fall in unit costs as the result of monopolization

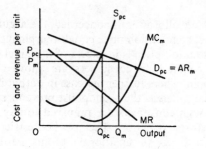

Figure 5

In this case more is produced at a lower price as the result of monopolization consequent on the reduced costs of large-scale production.

moves the marginal cost curve of the monopolist to the right of the original supply curve so that more is now produced at a lower price, as shown. This is not to say, of course, that the monopolist could not further increase output and lower price were he not trying to maximize his profit. Such a position would not, however, be the result of a return to perfect competition.

The State is thus seen to have a very real role in this context. It must not automatically encourage the degree of competition in every situation, nor break down established productive units into smaller less efficient ones. Its policy should be to act where imperfection is felt to be detrimental, while retaining and controlling the efficiencies arising from large-scale production and single ownership.

The State is seen to have a further role if one questions the mechanism by which resources are allocated in a free market. Increased consumer demand manifests itself in higher price. The owners of capital see the prospect of greater profit if they increase the production of the good. In order to do this they transfer inputs to this production and this is again done by means of price differentials. The consumer is provided with what he wanted through the agency of private profit. (The reader should be aware that he is dealing with two markets here; the market for the good, and the market for the factors which produce the good. The various forms we are examining are associated with both and a very real difficulty arises as we consider the effectiveness of 'freedom' in markets which are not perfect. The restrictive practices of all types of labour serve both to illustrate the point and act as their own warning to those who believe in the effectiveness of 'the market place' in the real world.) But private profit takes no account of the divergence which might exist between private and social revenues.

Private costs are those incurred by the individual firm and are measured by the value of the next best alternative use of the particular inputs involved in production, usually equivalent to their market price. Social costs are those incurred by the economy as a whole as the result of any economic decision and are measured in terms of the alternative use society has for these and any further resources affected. This is perhaps best explained by example. The cost to a tanker company of washing out its oil tanks at sea is relatively small. We can accept that this is a beneficial use of resources from the economy's standpoint; it requires essential fuel as cheaply as possible. But even if the country could not find a better use for the resources involved in this particular action, there is the further point that should the oil be washed up on the country's beaches, it is involved in the cost of cleaning them and caring for wildlife. And this is a cost not considered by the tanker company. There will of course be cases where the use of resources is directly questionable in terms of the alternative use to which they could be put. A look at the ever changing skyline of central London indicates the obvious profit to be made from building large office blocks. Perhaps a better use of the limited resources of the construction industry would be the provision of homes for those of the community whose needs, however desperate, are not reinforced by the money necessary to transfer resources under a system based on the making of private profit.

Similarly private revenue is the revenue the firm obtains from selling its product, whereas social revenue is the money value of the gain to society from the production and consumption of that product. The revenue a contractor receives for building a clinic is likely to be less than the social revenue resulting from the better health throughout the area served by it.

Where there is divergence between private and social costs and revenues it is obvious that any allocation of resources based only on the interaction of private cost and revenue cannot be an optimum one from the point of view of the economy as a whole. The fact that it is

15

difficult to quantify and order social costs and revenues does not mean that the State should not consider them in taking an obvious responsibility here.

Two further points arise from the fact that that resource allocation depends basically on consumer demand. Is consumer sovereignty sacrosanct? Does the consumer know what is best for him? Further, consumer demand depends on the way income is distributed between different sections of the community. A particular allocation of resources will perhaps be best for the income distribution on which it depends, but could there not be a better distribution? 'Optimum' is now seen to be a relative rather than an absolute term. Again the State is seen to have responsibility, both in supplementing the result of free consumer choice (e.g. providing compulsory insurance for a wide range of risks), and in compensating for the variations in income resulting from the private ownership of capital.

(ii) Monopoly and the public interest

It is now time to consider those aspects of the monopoly situation which could be considered against the public interest, those which could be included in the category of detrimental imperfections. It has been shown that the monopolist receives supernormal profits by charging a higher price and producing less than, with his cost and revenue structure, is possible. It has also been shown that when economies of large-scale production exist the solution is not to break down the industry into a large number of small producers, even where this is technologically possible. In such cases pressure must be applied to increase output and lower price while retaining the efficiency of single ownership. Perhaps the easiest way to do this is to bring the monopoly directly under State control (see third case study).

The monopolist's power to receive supernormal profits lies with his ability to restrict entry to the industry. It is sometimes argued that anything the authorities can do to open the market will thus be beneficial. In particular is condemned the protection of a home industry by means of a tariff placed on cheap imports. It is often the case, however, that there are other motives involved in tariff policy, so that general and outright condemnation of tariffs cannot follow because it might help in the control of monopolies.

Price discrimination
The monopolist is sometimes able to increase his profit by dividing his market and charging discriminatory prices. It is possible that this

16

works against the public interest, but again price discrimination should not be condemned outright. There are circumstances where most people would accept it as being a fairer pricing policy than that of a single market price. Two standard examples illustrate this. It is decided by law that for a given nationwide service price discrimination shall not exist between different geographical areas. It is found that in some areas the service does not pay, and so it is withdrawn, despite the fact that consumers in these areas might be willing to pay more for its retention. Perhaps the policy of uniform pricing is wrong in these circumstances. The cost of State schooling, which is provided free for every child, is met from central government taxation and local rates. Taxation in this country is progressive and rates are, in theory, correlated with income, so that in effect the richer the individual the more he has to pay for the education of his children. But this is simply part of generally accepted government policy which endeavours to redistribute income in favour of the poorer sections of the community.

There are, however, many cases where price discrimination should be condemned. Perhaps the saddest examples occur where price discrimination is a further manifestation of more basic social discrimination. It is perhaps less worrying that the small village branch of a large retail chain takes advantage of its local monopoly to charge higher prices than prevail in the neighbouring town than that, for example, in a similar situation in America higher prices are sometimes found in the Negro and immigrant districts of the cities.

There are circumstances in which production is only possible if price discrimination takes place. How this is done under the profit motive is shown below (the alternative, state production at a loss will again involve price discrimination as the loss is covered by taxation which is progressive). Consider Figure 6. Given the average total cost and average revenue curves, at no level of output is it profitable to produce as unit costs are continuously in excess of price. If the market is divided so that those willing to pay a higher price are allowed to do so, it is possible that the extra revenue received will cover total costs. The reader should be able to see that this will in fact be the case if the area *abcd* is greater than the area *cgfe*.

The theory of monopoly is based on the assumption of profit maximization, and conclusions based on this assumption must be modified wherever it is not applicable. In particular it is possible that the very existence of a government committed to anti-monopoly legislation could ensure that profits are not maximized by the monopolist as he endeavours to avoid notice. Some economists, notably J. A. Schumpeter, argue in any case that the existence of supernormal profit, primarily associated with 'big business', is necessary to act as

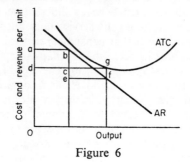

Figure 6

incentive to the innovator on whom economic growth ultimately depends. It must be noted that in the United Kingdom much research is undertaken by the government and also enough innovation stems from small units to suggest the need to qualify the above argument. Indeed it could be argued that, in as much as the competitor needs to innovate before his rivals and the monopolist is without this particular motive, the monopolist has less incentive to introduce new techniques or products. He does, however, have the incentive to innovate in that any profit he does make is likely to remain permanently. It is interesting to consider the patent laws in this context. They provide a quasi-monopolistic market for both large and small innovators, thus seeming to favour the latter. However, it is often said that it is the large-scale monopolist who benefits most as he may patent a process, thereafter to shelve it in case its introduction should upset the balance of his established position.

Finally, to break up a monopoly is most likely to give rise to an oligopolistic situation where the danger of joint action is very great, since ties between constituent parts of the industry already exist. The reader should consider the post-war history of the iron and steel industry in this context.

(iii) The wastes of monopolistic competition
The main feature of this market form, product differentiation, gives rise to a long-run equilibrium position of excess capacity. With its

18

given productive capacity each firm could produce more, at lower unit cost, but does not do so because it is committed to a policy of further differentiation of its product. It follows that resources are wasted as the output of an industry could be achieved with fewer constituent firms. The only government policy aimed at reducing excess capacity has been that of legislating against first group, and then individual enforcement of resale price maintenance, which leads to further excess capacity in the retail trade. Here it seems, the fact that the consumer might prefer to pay a higher price for more choice has been ignored in an attempt not to waste resources.

A concomitant disadvantage of product differentiation is the amount of resources devoted to competitive advertising, essentially a process of mutual cancellation. At the end of the 1960s the Monopolies Commission began to take an interest in the wastes of advertising, initially investigating the oligopolistic detergent industry (see Part 2). It remains to be seen if they will extend the policy, and if they will in fact be successful in such attempts to reduce this particular competitive waste wherever it occurs.

(iv) Oligopoly

In many circumstances unitary monopoly could be considered to be against the public interest. Empirical evidence suggests that there is opportunity and desire among oligopolists to act jointly in an endeavour to establish a group monopoly position which could also exhibit this property. It does not follow, however, that competition is automatically preferable, for the competitive costs of oligopoly involve a considerable waste of resources. There is the added fact that competition could lead to a price war which might cause disruption in the industry, to the obvious detriment of the consumer.

The legislator must, then, be aware of the harmful effects of both monopolistic and competitive actions on the part of the oligopolist. Thus there is legislation covering elimination of competition by various restrictive practices which may involve minimum price agreements as part of a policy of joint profit maximization, or action affecting the degree of competition elsewhere in the economy, as is the result on the retail trade of the enforcement of a uniform resale price, and at the same time legislation against the wastes of advertising expenditure.

Perhaps more should be done to eliminate the wastes of excess capacity caused by duplication of product, outlet or service. Anyone who has driven through the less salubrious areas of our Victorian cities, where a new petrol station is to be found on every other corner, must have thought about this.

Where there is mutual policy there must be agreement between firms. If the government decides that a monopolistic situation which is against the public interest has been developed, it simply forces the firms to break such agreements. It is obviously easier to recognize and legislate against formal agreements such as mergers, trusts and cartels,[1] than the less formal arrangements of price leadership, information agreement and tacit understanding.

The dominant firm

The above summary of the market forms did not specifically cover the situation where an industry has several producers but one dominant firm. This obviously approximates more to unitary monopoly than oligopoly, for it is likely that the smaller producers simply follow the policy laid down by the leading firm which need spend little time concerning itself with their expected or actual reactions. The possibility of a dominant firm using its power to lead the industry against the public interest is covered by the legislator's definition of monopoly. The policy of merger or take-over specifically to obtain a dominant position has also been covered by legislation (see Part 2).

It is sometimes the case that growth to a dominant position is the cumulative result of efficiency and the economies of large-scale production. In these circumstances a position of market dominance is not necessarily correlated with monopolistic practices, although the opportunity to misuse the power of such a position has been established. Wherever there are economies to be gained from large-scale production, and this is the situation in much manufacturing industry, it is likely that the more efficient firms will expand until there is a situation of oligopoly or market dominance by one firm. Both

---

[1] There has developed a wide range of associations as firms have sought to act to mutual advantage. A merger is a straightforward combination of two or more firms. Originally a trust was a form of combination where control of constituent companies was vested in the hands of a board of trustees, the company's shares being exchanged for trust certificates. In America the 1890 Sherman Act declared trusts illegal, and perhaps as a result of this the word is now used as a general derogatory name for any large combination exercising monopoly power. A cartel is a joint marketing organization established by firms which would otherwise sell in competition. A central 'syndicate' fixes selling prices and output quotas.

situations give rise to the opportunity for monopolistic practice.

(v) Final conclusion

The theories of the market forms outlined here suggest that there are features of monopoly, oligopoly and monopolistic competition which could be against the public interest. It is often difficult to decide under which heading a particular situation falls, and it cannot be emphasized enough that the theories (and where they have not been fully developed, the empirical evidence) only give rise to features within each market form which *could* be considered detrimental to the public good. With such knowledge of the abuses which are likely to be found, however, one is in a more informed position to consider each case on its own merits.

SELECTED QUESTIONS

The questions below are taken from G.C.E. advanced level and university entrance examinations.

1. Examine the limits to the exercise of monopoly power. (*London*)
2. Is the number of firms in an industry a good indication of the strength of the producers' monopoly? (*London*)
3. Are high profits a good indication of the strength of monopoly power? Explain your answer. (*London*)
4. Why are public utilities such as electricity, gas, and water usually monopolies? (*London*)
5. What is a 'discriminating monopolist'? In what circumstances could one operate successfully? (*Cambridge*)
6. Why do airlines offer much lower fares to members of clubs travelling in large groups? (*Cambridge*)
7. Should the economists' theory of profit maximizing firms be abandoned because the assumption of profit maximization is unrealistic? Explain your answer. (*London*)
8. What are the *disadvantages* of a free price system as the only means of allocating resources? (*London*)
9. Analyse the effects on the price and output of a commodity that will be brought about if the industry producing it is transformed from a state of perfect competition to one of monopoly. (*Cambridge*)
10. What reasons are there to believe that prices would be lower if an industry were working under conditions of perfect competition than if the industry were working under conditions of monopoly?

(*Cambridge*)

PART 2
MONOPOLY LEGISLATION

INTRODUCTION

This section gives a fairly detailed account of British experience with monopoly and restrictive practice legislation in the period after the Second World War. It traces the development from the 1948 Act through to the Restrictive Trade Practices Act introduced in the House of Commons by the President of the Board of Trade in 1968. From 1948 until the Act of 1956 the legislation is dealt with chronologically but then each part of the 1956 Act is followed through separately in order to cover further developments in each area before the 1973 Fair Trading Act brought together all aspects of monopoly, mergers, restrictive practices, and consumer protection into one piece of legislation. The structure of the legislation is seen in the diagram below:

1948 Monopolies and Restrictive Practices (Inquiry and Control) Act.

1949 Patents Act.

1953 Monopolies and Restrictive Practices Act (amending the 1948 Act).

1956 Restrictive Trade Practices Act.

Part One	*Part Two*	*Part Three*
Established the Registrar of Restrictive Practices and the R.P. Court.	Banned collective resale price maintenance.	Reduced the strength of the Monopolies Commission.
1968 Restrictive Trade Practices Act.	1964 Resale Prices Act.	1965 Monopolies and Mergers Act.

1973 Fair Trading Act. Consumer protection specifically included.

1. EARLY ATTEMPTS TO CONTROL MONOPOLY AND RESTRICTIVE PRACTICES

'Combinations in restraint of trade' are centuries old but nation-wide agreements were not widespread until the last quarter of the nineteenth century. Equally there have been laws against monopolies and restrictive practices for centuries but these were largely ineffective. By the end of the last century the Courts appear to have laid emphasis on 'freedom of contract' rather than 'freedom of trade'. Contracts were upheld in the Courts even though they restricted trade. Even before the First World War restrictive agreements existed in a wide variety of manufacturing industries. During the war itself, the growth of agreements accelerated.

Immediately after the war the government was hostile to monopolies and restrictive practices. The Committee on Trusts (1919) and Committees of Enquiry under the Profiteering Acts 1919–20 focused attention on the great increase in the arrangements for restricting competition and fixing prices. In 1920 a Monopolies Bill was actually drafted. However, the Depression provided a powerful justification for the acceptance of trade agreements intended to stabilize prices and reduce surplus productive capacity. It was felt that such restrictive agreements might help as a defence against the depression. New and complex arrangements began to appear and these often involved sanctions imposed by private trade courts, e.g. fines and stop lists. Furthermore some industries began to press for state support for their schemes, e.g. the railways in 1921.

These schemes of rationalization upon which manufacturers embarked took many forms but were almost invariably directed towards one or more of three ends: (1) restriction on entry to the trade; (2) price fixing; (3) the reduction of productive capacity. Such agreements occurred in industries including coal, cotton and ship-building.

Moves towards the creation of private monopolies through amalgamation, e.g. The Distillers' Company (1925) and I.C.I. (1926), received official support in a variety of ways and a number of Statutory Schemes were passed, e.g. road passenger transport and agricultural marketing.[1] During the Depression the courts were well-disposed towards contracts in 'restraint of trade' and the government, in

---

[1] J. W. Grove, *Government and Industry in Britain*, p. 46.

encouraging the policy of rationalization, aided the spread of restrictive practices.

The position at the end of the Second World War

At first sight it appeared, at the end of the war, that the trade associations and dominant firms were going to consolidate their already influential position. During the war these had become very useful agents for implementing government policy and in the later stages of the war the government had consulted with the associations on plans for reconstruction afterwards. The Board of Trade set up working parties to examine a wide range of industries and all recommended that representative bodies should be set up in every industry. To give effect to this recommendation the Industrial Organization and Development Act (1947) was passed creating in a number of industries representative associations with authority to raise compulsory levies and to undertake a variety of technical and commercial activities.

However the first clear sign that the government intended to take action against monopolies and restrictive practices came with the publication of the White Paper on 'Employment Policy in 1944'.[1] Circumstances had changed. The work of J. M. Keynes had thrown light on the problems of controlling the economy and for the first time the government had accepted responsibility for maintaining full employment. In the 1944 White Paper the government stated that employers and employees would have to abandon restrictive practices to allow the economy to expand and to maintain employment at the required level. The government was aware of the problems posed by restrictive practices (probably based on wartime experience) but did not at this stage, draw up a framework for legislation.

In the following years a number of *ad hoc* Committees of Inquiry were set up in industries where monopoly and restrictive practices

---

[1] 'Employers too, must seek in larger output rather than in higher prices the reward of enterprise and good management. There has been in recent years a growing tendency towards combines and towards agreements, both national and international, to divide markets and to fix conditions of sale. Such agreements do not necessarily operate against the public interest: but the power to do so is there. The government will therefore seek power to inform themselves of the extent and effect of restrictive agreements, and of the activities of combines; and to take appropriate action to check practices which may bring advantages to sectional producing interests but work to the detriment of the country as a whole.'

were suspected, e.g. radio valves, cotton textile machinery, cement-building materials and components, Welsh slate industry, and the Lloyd Jacob Committee reported on Resale Price Maintenance. Such reports drew attention to the problem but as yet there was little indication of its extent or severity. But then an article in the Journal of the Royal Statistical Society in 1945 by H. Leak and A. Maizels showed a very high degree of concentration in British industry.

In view of their evidence that monopolies and restrictive practices were fairly widespread there was an increasing demand for detailed and continuous observation of the effects of these practices in the light of the public interest. Britain, in her weakened international economic position, could not neglect any means of increasing her competitive power. Furthermore Britain had accepted the obligations in the Havana Charter for an International Trade Organization (1948) to attack monopolies and restrictive practices.[1]

2. THE 1948 MONOPOLIES AND RESTRICTIVE PRACTICES (INQUIRY AND CONTROL) ACT

The first step in the control of monopoly was taken in 1948 when the Monopolies and Restrictive Practices (Inquiry and Control) Act was passed. This outlined the procedures by which such practices could be investigated. The government stated that there was an urgent need to investigate whether the powers of monopolists and parties to restrictive arrangements *were* being used against the public interest and if it were shown that they were, 'effective and appropriate steps' were to be taken 'to curb any of these anti-social practices'.

It has been pointed out elsewhere[2] that the 1948 Act was much more successful in its inquiries than in bringing the practices under control. The Act enabled the facts about monopolies and restrictive practices to be exposed and the subsequent reports provided a focus for discussion: additional information was forthcoming from a variety of sources. For the first time a body of information was becoming available on restrictive industrial agreements.

The Act comprised some twenty-two sections. It began by setting up a Monopolies Commission of not less than four and not more than ten members, then defined the situations to which the Act applied and

---

[1] See P. H. Guenault and J. M. Jackson, *The Control of Monopoly in the United Kingdom*, ch. 4.

[2] J. W. Grove, *Government and Industry in Britain*, ch. 7.

the duties of the Commission investigating and reporting on these situations. It continued by providing for remedial action which might be taken following such reports. The Act finally provided for special investigation into the practices themselves.

The Board of Trade alone had the power to initiate inquiries into monopolies and restrictive practices by referring cases to the Monopolies Commission. Although it has no formal powers of initiation there is nothing to prevent the Commission from making informal suggestions to the Board of Trade. The Board may refer cases to the Commission where it appears that 'conditions to which the Act applies, prevail'. The Commission then investigates and reports back to the Board; it has no power to deal with any practices it deems to be operating against the public interest. Instead the Commission makes recommendations to the Board of Trade as to the action it considers necessary. The Board is in no way obliged to act on these recommendations.

The government recognized the difficulty in defining monopoly and it is significant that the term was not used in the Act except in the title and preamble. Instead the Act took market dominance as its criterion. The Act was to apply when at least one-third of all the goods supplied or processed in the U.K., or in any substantial part of the U.K., were supplied to or processed by any person, or two or more persons being inter-connected bodies corporate (a firm plus subsidiaries).

According to Guenault and Jackson the government had attempted to find a legal definition of the 'public interest' but had failed, leaving the Monopolies Commission free to formulate its own interpretation of the term.[1] The Act referred to public interest only in terms of efficient and full utilization of resources, the encouragement of new types of enterprise and technique, and the provision of the right types of good.[2]

There is no doubt that a good deal was left to the discretion of the Board of Trade. The interpretation of the Act gives rise to considerable problems: the definition of a 'class of goods'; the measurement of the share of the market; the interpretation of such phrases as 'a substantial part of the U.K.'. The Act illustrates some of the difficulties of approaching the control of monopolies and restrictive

---

[1] Guenault and Jackson, p. 38.

[2] For a discussion on the guidance given by the 1948 Act see, *The British Monopolies Commission*, C. K. Rowley, p. 72.

practices from a legal point of view. The 1948 Act does not apply to Nationalized Industries or statutory bodies, e.g. the Agricultural Marketing Boards, nor does it apply to Trade Unions. Services, the supply of services and service trades likewise are not included.

If the Commission found that monopoly conditions existed and were operating against the public interest then the government could make an Order declaring the agreements or arrangements in the industry to be unlawful and requiring parties to these agreements to end them. Frequently the Minister sought to have the Commission's findings accepted voluntarily by the industry concerned. In such cases the government accepted assurances from the parties that the practices concerned would be modified. The Board of Trade could then refer to the Commission the question whether and to what extent the assurances had been fulfilled. Since 1948 only one such follow-up investigation has been carried out: the 1958 follow-up report on the supply of imported timber. In this case it was found that very little had been done to meet the assurances given to the Board of Trade. This failure to follow up cases where assurances have been given emphasizes the weakness of this approach. Manufacturers who give such assurances to the Board may well continue with their practices since the risk of detection from a follow-up investigation is so slight, and no penalties are incurred by such manufacturers if they are found out.

The Board of Trade's choice of references was guided by a desire to investigate many different types of restrictive practice as well as trades or industries which raised fresh problems.[1] This was done in order to provide a wide range of experience for future needs. The Board has been criticized for showing 'a staggering lack of imagination' in its choice of industries.[2] Certainly the industries investigated did not arouse any great public interest. Most of the references were concerned with raw materials and capital goods, and with cartels rather than unitary monopoly.

Between 1948 and 1956 twenty reports were produced on individual industries and a further report, based on a general reference, was made on Collective Discrimination in 1955. The Commission's reports revealed a wide variety of practices: some designed to protect a monopoly position by hindering competition, e.g. discriminatory rebates, collective boycotts and exclusive dealing; other practices,

---

[1] See Guenault and Jackson, ch. 6.
[2] P. Donaldson, *Guide to the British Economy*, p. 90.

including common prices, common conditions of sale, output and sales quotas, and collective resale price maintenance, were designed to exploit a monopoly position. The Commission found that in only one industry (the manufacture and supply of insulin) were none of the practices investigated contrary to the public interest. However, the Board usually accepted assurances from the parties that the practices would be modified and, when it was seen that follow-up investigations were extremely rare, manufacturers usually did nothing.

3. THE 1949 PATENTS ACT

In 1949 the Patents Act was passed: this took account of restrictive practices resulting from the use of patents (previously excluded from the Monopoly Commission's powers). If the Monopolies Commission found that restrictive conditions contained in a patent licence were harmful, or likely to be so, the government could declare these contrary to the public interest and could cancel or modify the conditions of the licence. Only once since 1949 has this been done. The Ministry of Health, faced with paying extremely high prices for certain drugs from British and American patent holders, invoked section 46 of the Patents Act which enables any government department 'to make, use and exercise any patented invention for the services of the Crown'. The Ministry of Health in an attempt to cut the cost of the national drug bill, invited tenders for a supply of tetracycline to hospitals operating under the N.H.S. Neither those tendering nor the manufacturer were licensed by the patent-holder Pfizer Corporation. Pfizer's were quoting a price of £80 to chemists and £45 per thousand tablets to hospitals. The firm whose tender was accepted by the Ministry of Health was charging £4 per thousand tablets.

The Pfizer Corporation, an American Company, challenged the legality of the Minister's action. The case was finally taken to the House of Lords where it was upheld in February 1965, that the Minister of Health was acting within his rights, when he purchased drugs from the non-licensed firms. However, in October 1965 the Minister of Health started buying from Pfizer's again at a higher price than that charged by the drug pirates. This was done in order to encourage British drug manufacturers to maintain their research programmes. Such programmes would have suffered if the Minister continued to buy from abroad from pirates who had no development costs to cover. The Minister of Health was successful in forcing

Pfizer's and other drug firms to reduce the prices of their products to the Health Service.[1]

4. 1953 MONOPOLIES AND RESTRICTIVE PRACTICES ACT

In 1953 a Monopolies and Restrictive Practices Act was passed, which was intended to strengthen the Commission and speed up its progress. The maximum membership was increased from 10 to 25, and the post of chairman was made permanent, and in addition three deputy chairmen were appointed. The 1953 Act allowed the Commission to divide into sub-committees[2] thus helping to speed up its investigations by permitting it to investigate and report on several references simultaneously.

The Commission in its work made it clear that restrictive agreements existed in many industries and in many different forms.[3] However, without compulsory registration of such agreements it was impossible to say how numerous they were. Furthermore in the absence of such information it was impossible to assess the damage that such agreements inflicted on the economy. While the direct results of the 1948 Act were very limited, through its inquiries knowledge of the various practices increased significantly as did understanding of the problems of assessing their effects.

In 1952 the Commission received a 'general reference' to report on collective discrimination (exclusive dealing, collective boycotts and aggregated rebates, etc.). In 1955 the Commission reported. The report was unusual in that it contained a majority and a minority recommendation. The majority felt that collective discrimination was against the public interest and should be made illegal except in a few special cases. The minority recommended that all agreements should be registered and, after individual consideration, those found to be against the public interest should be dissolved.

---

[1] In March 1966 I.C.I. entered the market in an attempt to break Pfizer's monopoly in the supply of particular antibiotics. Pfizer's patent for oxytetracycline expired at the end of February 1966 and in March I.C.I. began selling this drug at prices about two-thirds lower than Pfizers. See *Time & Tide*, 24–30th March, 1966.

[2] These groups were to consist of not less than 5 members.

[3] See Alex Hunter, 'The Control of Monopoly', *Lloyds Bank Review*, Oct. 1956.

5. 1956 RESTRICTIVE TRADE PRACTICES ACT

In this Act the government compromised by borrowing from the views of both sides of the 1955 Commission Report. The Act separated the investigation of restrictive practices from that of monopoly. Restrictive Practices were to be dealt with through the new Restrictive Practices Court, a Court of law whose decisions were to be binding, while monopolies were still to be dealt with by a newly established Commission which was still only empowered to report and recommend.

The Act fell into three parts:

Part One dealt with the registration and judicial investigation of restrictive practices.

Part Two dealt with resale price maintenance.

Part Three was concerned with the Monopolies Commission.

Each part of the 1956 Act will now be covered separately and each is subsequently developed in order to consider recent legislation or proposed legislation alongside the appropriate section of the 1956 Act.

(i) Part One of the 1956 Act – Restrictive Practices

This provided for the compulsory registration of a wide range of agreements relating to the production and sale of goods, with the Registrar of the new Restrictive Practices Court. The Act did not cover practices in service trades or transport. All agreements between two or more producers or suppliers of goods involving restrictions in respect of prices, quantities, descriptions, terms, places and conditions of trading were to be registered. It was immaterial whether the agreements were oral or not, or whether or not they were intended to be enforceable at law. Such registration is only a preliminary: the agreements are then brought before the Restrictive Practices Court. Initially all agreements are assumed to operate against the public interest. This is the reverse of usual English legal practice where parties are assumed to be innocent until proved guilty. If, however, the parties to the agreement could satisfy the Court that it was not against the public interest then the agreement would be permitted (thus partially satisfying the minority demand). The responsibility for deciding upon the agreements to receive early attention rested with the Board of Trade.[1] In April 1957 the Registrar was instructed to start proceedings relating to eleven commodities.[2] Between 1957 and 1958 the Board gave further directions covering 63 commodities. However, in October 1958 these directions were rescinded leaving the Registrar free to select the cases.

The Restrictive Practices Court is composed of five High Court Judges assisted by ten Lay Assessors.[3] It comprises five Divisions: three in England, one in Scotland and one in Northern Ireland. Each consists of one judge and at least two lay assessors. The Registrar is empowered to bring agreements before the court which then decides whether or not the agreement is contrary to the public interest.[4] All agreements are assumed initially to be against the public interest and the onus of proving otherwise falls on the parties to the agreement. All agreements remain on the register even after they have been cancelled except those considered by the Board of Trade to be of no great economic significance.

At the outset agreements are assumed to operate against the public interest but the Court may uphold any restriction which can 'jump' two hurdles. Firstly the parties must show that the agreement does meet the needs of any one of the 'Seven Gateways' (see below), and having done this, it must be shown that the agreement is not unreasonable: that the benefits felt by the public due to the agreement should exceed the detriment to the public resulting from the maintenance of the agreement. This second hurdle has become known as the 'Tailpiece', and unless the restriction jumps this double hurdle it is declared to be against the public interest. An agreement, or part of an

---

[1] Subsequently this responsibility was transferred to the Registrar in October 1958.

[2] Bread, corrugated paper, cotton yarns, hard-fibre cordage, semi-manufactures of high conductivity copper, proprietary medicines, school milk, steel boilers, structural steelwork.

[3] The Act provides that on matters of law the opinion of the presiding judge shall prevail but that on matters of fact the opinion of the Court shall be the majority opinion.

[4] The Registrar is not a public prosecutor: he merely notifies the Court that the agreement exists, the parties to the agreement then present their case in an attempt to show that it is not against the public interest. The Registrar must ensure the Court has all the relevant information, so that the Court can decide whether or not the agreement operates against the public interest.

agreement, that is found contrary to the public interest is void and must be dissolved and the Court may issue an injunction to give effect to this if it thinks fit. (See the case of the Aluminium Manufacturers Jan. 1968.)

The parties to the agreement must show that it confers benefits through one or more of the following 'Seven Gateways':[1]

The Seven Gateways
1. by protecting the public against injury in connection with the installation, use or consumption of goods;
2. by making available other 'specific and substantial' benefits to the public;
3. by counteracting restrictive measures taken by 'any one person' who is not a party to the agreement;
4. by permitting the negotiation of 'fair terms' for the purchase or sale of goods, with buyers or sellers who represent a predominant part of the trade;
5. by preventing the occurrence of 'serious and persistent' unemployment in an area heavily dependent upon the particular trade;
6. in maintaining the volume or earnings of the export trade in the commodity where this is substantial in relation to the export trade of the U.K. as a whole or in relation to the whole business of the particular trade;
7. in maintaining some other restriction which the Court holds to be justified on its own merits.

Some industries are covered by a few agreements, e.g. cement, carpets and paint, while other industries including building, iron and steel, and textiles have more than 150 agreements. The majority of agreements on the register are between manufacturers and deal with selling prices. Some agreements contain more than 100 restrictions.[2]

As with the 1948 Monopolies Act difficulty was experienced with the precise meaning of the 'public interest'. Consequently no actual

---

[1] See page 53 for provisions of the 1968 Act including an additional 'gateway'.

[2] It is quite common to find that the Registrar has referred several different agreements to the Restrictive Practices Court all relating to the same industry or trade, e.g. of the 63 Agreements referred to the Court at the end of March 1967, 7 related to Sunday Newspapers, 5 to fish and 4 to furniture agreements.

definition of the term appears in the 1956 Act either. J. Wiseman points out that the Restrictive Practices Court appears to have identified the public interest with the *absence of the conditions* set out in paragraph 6 of the Act which defines a registrable agreement.[1]

It is essential that the Court should be able to have all the relevant facts and opinions, consequently the Registrar is authorized, if necessary, to investigate costs and bring such evidence before the Court. The rules concerning evidence are wider than those which apply in ordinary courts and it can consider the evidence of the Monopolies Commission and economists. If an agreement is declared to be against the public interest and is dissolved, the Court may issue an order preventing the parties from making any other to like effect. The Court may prohibit some of the restrictions in any agreement yet authorize others.

The Registration Order took effect in November 1956 and the following table shows subsequent development:

Date		No. of agreements registered
February	1957	Approx. 800
August	1957	1,700
June	1959	2,200
August	1960	2,300
June	1961	2,350
June	1963	2,430
June	1966	2,550
October	1969	3,000

Of the 2,300 registered agreements in 1960, 1,030 had been abandoned, 970 of them without reference to the Court, and 26 agreements had been removed from the register as being of no significant economic importance. Sixty-three cases had been referred to the Restrictive Practices Court but of these only eleven were contested before full Court proceedings, i.e. 52 cases were not defended and were subsequently dissolved. In only one case up to this time 1960 was the agreement upheld completely, the Water Tube Boilers' Agreement, while in two other cases certain particulars were upheld: the remaining restrictions being outlawed. These were the Black Nut and Bolt Agreement and the Blanket Manufacturers' Agreement.

---

[1] J. Wiseman, 'Economic Analysis and Public Policy', *E.J.*, September, 1960.

	June 1963	1966
Cases referred to Court and disposed of or in the course of preparation:	160	280
Agreements modified or expired and not referred to Court:	1,505	1,875
Agreements being considered as of no economic significance:	185	130
Agreements probably dependent on cases currently referred to Court:	150	50
Miscellaneous Balance	430	215
NUMBER OF AGREEMENTS REGISTERED	2,430	2,550

Up to June 1963 when there were 2,430 Agreements registered, 1,000 of these had been brought to an end by the parties to the agreement and a further 525 had been so varied as to remove all the restrictions with which the Act is concerned. By the end of June 1966 of the 2,550 registered agreements, 1,135 had been brought to an end by the parties (either before or after reference to the Court) and a further 840 had been varied thus removing them from the scope of the Act. In addition, a further 75 agreements had expired and were not renewed. Thus the total number of agreements which had been terminated by act of the parties, by expiration or by modification of agreement was 2,110 at the end of June 1966. The corresponding figure for June 1963 was 1,610. Up to the end of March 1967 only 35 cases had been contested before full Court proceedings and in only 11 have agreements been upheld.[1] The most frequently used 'Gateway' was 'specific and substantial benefits to the public'. This proved to be successful in eight out of the eleven successful cases. The Fish Price Agreement was the most recent case in which this 'Gateway' was successful (November 9th 1966). At the end of March 1967 there were 63 agreements referred to the Court including some which had been on the register for several years while the Aluminium Semi-Manufactures Agreement was only recently transferred from the Monopolies Commission.[2]

---

[1] Cases not contrary to the public interest:
Water Tube Boilers, Black Nut and Bolt, Cement, Permanent Magnets, Metal Windows, Net Books, Sulphur, Steel Scrap, Glazed Tiles, Black Nut and Bolt (New Agreement), Fish.

[2] In September 1966 it was decided the agreement came under the jurisdiction of the Registrar and the Court not under the Commission.

In his report presented to Parliament in January 1967, the Registrar drew attention to the fact that less than 1 per cent of the registered agreements, whether made before or after the passing of the Act, have been found consistent with the public interest. In the great majority of cases, when faced with the task of defending the agreements, the parties to the agreement have either ended or modified them. This applies to both pre-Act and post-Act agreements. Increasingly the Registrar has had to resort to enforcement procedure to compel firms to register their agreements. In his first report published in 1959 only 10 per cent of the registrations were the result of enforcement procedure whereas of the 145 agreements added to the register in the period 1963–67, 75 per cent were the result of enforcement procedure.

A survey of Part One of the 1956 Act

At the time when the Act was passed it was not known how many agreements would be registered or how many cases would be defended in court. The small number of cases that have been defended tends to create the impression that not much progress has been made, but this is very misleading. A very large number of agreements have been modified or abandoned as a result of the few cases heard by the court and this has led to several developments. A new type of open-price agreement has become widespread.[1] It was at this time very difficult to deal with such information agreements.[2] Moreover there has been in the late 1950's and early 1960's a movement towards mergers and monopolies. Indeed at the time of the passing of the Act, it was predicted that such a movement would take place. It is reasoned that since the Monopolies Commission is slower in its investigations and many of the Commissions recommendations are ignored there is less chance of government interference from this source than from the Restrictive Practices Court. Furthermore there is much less of a chance of a follow-up investigation from the Commission. Between 1948–1967, as we have seen, there has been only one follow-up investigation by the Commission, the 1958 Inquiry into Imported Timber.

---

[1] Prior to the 1956 Act the British Starter Battery Association operated a common battery price agreement but abandoned it due to the 'climate of legislation' of the 1956 Act. From 1960 the B.S.B.A. substituted exchange of information among its members.

[2] The 1968 Act makes provision for the registration of such information agreements.

In contrast the Registrar and the Court worked quickly and few agreements were successfully upheld. In addition there have already been two 'follow-up cases' (in fact the cases were heard within thirteen months of each other, May 1965 and June 1966). In the case of the Galvanized Tank Manufacturers' Agreement the eight companies involved were fined a total of £102,000 for contempt of Court in that they continued to operate agreements declared to be against the public interest.[1] The President of the Court said that imprisonment for such contempt of Court should be considered in future cases. In June 1966 the Mileage Conference Group of the Tyre Manufacturers' Conference was found guilty of contempt of Court and the eight firms were fined a total of £80,000.[2] The firms contended that legal opinion they had received indicated their modified agreement was permissible. In this context the penalty imposed by the Court was more lenient than it would otherwise have been.

The Registrar's Review, February 1967
The Registrar in reviewing the position under the 1956 Act noted that certain weaknesses had developed in the decade since the Act was passed:

1. There was a good chance that if an agreement was registered and brought to the Court it would be declared to be against the public interest and made illegal and if the parties continued to operate it they may well be found guilty of contempt of Court and fined heavily. On the other hand if the parties to the agreement did not even register the agreement in the first place they incurred no penalty whatsoever. The parties operated the agreement until the Registrar initiates enforcement procedure. Thus of the new registrations three-quarters were the direct result of such enforcement since firms realized that they had nothing to lose and everything to gain by not registering.

2. The 1956 definition of an agreement which must be registered was not wide enough to include all information agreements. Thus many new types of information agreement were being used in place of the price agreements which had been condemned or abandoned by virtue of the Act. Although some such agreements were already registrable many were not.

3. Some agreements can be made and operated for a considerable

---

[1] July 1959.

[2] The earlier agreement was declared to operate against the public interest in October 1961.

time against the public interest even though the parties to such agreements frequently have no intention of attempting a defence of the agreement.

4. When the Court finds an agreement to operate against the public interest it makes an order declaring it to be illegal. The Registrar however felt that the order which is made by the Court may well be too narrow to prevent the parties making another agreement which is just as restrictive as the one declared illegal. When the Court finds a restriction contrary to the public interest, the agreement or that part of it becomes void, and the Court may make such order as appears necessary for restraining any parties to the agreement from using it or from making 'any other agreement to the like effect'. However, there is no great difficulty in drafting agreements in various ways so that the obligations imposed look different whereas in fact and in intention the practical results to be achieved are the same.

5. The Registrar felt that his obligation to refer all registered agreements to the Court is unnecessary and wasteful in relation to a substantial number of agreements which have been abandoned by the parties before the reference. The House of Lords decided in December 1963 that all agreements entered in the register were to be referred to the Restrictive Practices Court and the Registrar was charged with the duty of taking proceedings before the Court in respect of all such agreements. At the end of January 1967 there were 1,875 agreements which were not operative, some have been abandoned for up to eight years. The Registrar saw little advantage in referring such cases to the Court. *N.B.* the provisions of the 1968 Restrictive Trade Practices Act.

Events leading to the 1968 Restrictive Trade Practices Act
By the middle 1960s most of the formal price-fixing agreements had been dissolved and there was no backlog of important agreements awaiting reference to the Court. Following the publication of the Registrar's report in January 1967, there was a great deal of public discussion on restrictive practices.[1]

Mr. Douglas Jay, President of the Board of Trade, announced in the Commons in February 1967, that the Government was to extend and strengthen the 1956 Act, in an amending Bill to be introduced in a later session of Parliament.[2] He stated that the 1956 Act had made

---

[1] See Malcolm Crawford, 'Restrictive Practices – Wind of Change', *Statist*, 27th January, 1967.

[2] Subsequently this became the 1968 Restrictive Trade Practices Act.

'an important contribution to a more competitive climate in British industry and commerce' but that it was in need of amendment. Mr. Jay indicated that the new Bill would bring information agreements within its scope. During 1967 the Government received proposals from the N.E.D.C., the Confederation of British Industry and of course from the Registrar of Restrictive Practices, Mr. Sich.

In January 1968 Mr. Justice Megaw, presiding over the Restrictive Practices Court, took the unusual course of issuing injunctions forbidding Britain's seven leading aluminium companies to make pricing pacts or attempting to continue an agreement which they had decided not to defend. The companies had offered to observe a Court Order outlawing the price agreement which they had observed for ten years in breach of the 1956 Act. For ten years these companies had met periodically at informal meetings to discuss price changes. No minutes or records of these meetings were kept. Eventually in 1966 the agreement was registered with the Registrar but in the Restrictive Practices Court the parties did not seek to defend it. The Court had been given no explanation as to why the agreement had not been registered and consequently could not accept the undertakings given by the companies.

Again towards the end of January 1968 the first-ever criminal prosecution under the 1956 Restrictive Trade Practices Act – against two firms which dominate the supply of traffic-light equipment – opened at the Old Bailey. The companies, Automatic and Telephone Electric and G.E.C. Road Signals, were charged with suppressing details of their price-fixing agreements and giving false information to the Registrar of Restrictive Trading Agreements. The firms were subsequently fined a total of £1,000 for suppressing details of their price pact.

The Times leader on January 29th 1968 commented 'For seven years the Registrar . . . has been drawing attention to deficiencies in the law covering the investigation of price-fixing pacts. That groups of manufacturers and suppliers attempt and sometimes succeed in delaying court investigations is clearly not due to any lack of vigilance by Mr. Sich and his staff.

'These two different cases [referring to the aluminium manufacturers and the traffic-light equipment companies] serve as a timely reminder to the Government that amending legislation cannot be long delayed. Changes to the Act were, after all, foreshadowed by the Board of Trade nearly twelve months ago.'

One proposal put forward would give third parties damaged by the operation of restrictive agreements the power to seek civil remedies from the Courts as is the case in America. At that time three giant American drug manufacturers, who were each fined the maximum sum of £150,000 in December 1967 for monopolistic practices in violation of the Sherman Anti-Trust Law, were facing civil suits well in excess of $100m.

6. 1968 RESTRICTIVE TRADE PRACTICES ACT

This Act which was passed at the end of October exempted certain agreements which had previously been registrable under Part I of the 1956 Act. These exemptions related to agreements of importance to the national economy. Such agreements have to show:

1. that the agreement is calculated to promote the carrying out of an industrial or commercial project or scheme of substantial importance;
2. that its object or main object is to promote efficiency in a trade or industry or to create or improve productive capacity in an industry;
3. that this object cannot be achieved or achieved within a reasonable time except by means of the agreement or of an agreement for similar purposes;
4. that no relevant restrictions are accepted under the agreement other than such as are reasonably necessary to achieve that object; and
5. that the agreement is on balance expedient in the national interest.

A further provision of the Act makes it possible for the Board of Trade, and certain other departments, to exempt from registration agreements which include provisions designed to prevent or restrict price increases or to secure reductions in those prices. The Act applies to any recommendation made by a trade association.

It can be seen that in (2) above an attempt has been made to adopt a more flexible approach. Over the past few years the I.R.C. has been urging firms to merge and adopt a more rational structure in the interests of greater efficiency. The 1968 Act recognizes this development and consequently firms which merged under such directions need no longer fear having to defend their actions.

Clause 5 of the Act requires any class of 'information agreement' to be registered – thus implementing one of the Registrar's main proposals from the 1967 Report. Such information agreements must be registered within a time limit of three months in most cases. Failure to register now means that parties to such agreements are liable to actions 'for breach of statutory duty'.

A further suggestion proposed by the Registrar has also been acted upon: the Registrar is now given discretionary powers in deciding upon the agreements that need to be taken before the Restrictive Practices Court. No longer is he required to take all agreements before the Court. *The Times* reported (4th October, 1969) that the 'Board of Trade has cleared ten trade agreements registered under the 1968 Restrictive Trade Practices Act, and has used its power under Section 9 of the Act to discharge the Registrar from the duty of taking proceedings. This has been done under the rather more flexible provision in the Act relating to agreements of "no substantial economic significance".'

In addition the 1968 Act added a further 'Gateway' to the seven already in existence under Part I of the 1956 Act (see page 32). This eighth gateway states:

'that the restriction does not directly or indirectly restrict or discourage competition to any material degree in any relevant trade or industry and is not likely to do so.'

It must be remembered that firms wishing to justify their agreements must still jump the double hurdle – passing through one of the gateways is one of stages but firms still need to satisfy the requirement of the 'tailpiece' (see page 31).

(ii) Part Two of the 1956 Act – Resale Price Maintenance

In 1949 the Lloyd Jacob Committee reported. This was an *ad hoc* Committee set up to investigate resale price maintenance. The Committee pointed out that the demand for R.P.M. frequently came from the retailer since many traders were not strongly organized and to sell at a fixed price meant that their profit margin was assured.[1] R.P.M. prevented cut-throat competition and the elimination of many traders. The Lloyd Jacob Report recommended that although Individual R.P.M. should be allowed (it has been maintained that an individual manufacturer has a 'right' to determine the price at which his product is sold). Collective R.P.M. should be made illegal. There were cases.

---

[1] See Margaret Hall *Distributive Trading* for the results of Cadbury's pre-war trading experience.

e.g. the tyre trade, where to enforce Collective R.P.M., representatives of the Association went round to members to make 'test purchases' to see whether distributors were conforming to the agreed prices on new and remould tyres; where the distributors were found to be selling at below the fixed price they were called to account for their actions in front of a private Trade Court composed of members of the Association. Stop lists and fines were the most frequent sentences imposed. The Monopolies Commission reporting on the Supply and Export of Pneumatic Tyres in 1955–6 recommended that both individual and collective R.P.M. should be made illegal in this trade.

The workings of Part II of the 1956 Act

Part II of the 1956 Act made it legal for an individual seller to enforce resale prices not only against the first buyer but against others subsequently acquiring the goods in the course of trade for the purpose of selling them, provided the latter were given notice of the resale price conditions. This added the force of law to Individual R.P.M. since manufacturers could now take offending distributors to court. Collective R.P.M. however was now prohibited: it was made illegal for a number of suppliers to agree to withhold goods, or impose discriminatory terms or penalties on distributors who had not maintained resale prices.

During the period 1956–65 some manufacturers waived their right to fix maximum prices though frequently this was only for short periods which often coincided with a slackening of demand for the trade concerned, e.g. refrigerators. To this extent therefore some price competition was found in the retail trade.[1] However, in 1960 Professor B. S. Yamey estimated that a quarter of personal consumer expenditure was still on price maintained goods.[2]

In the period prior to the 1964 Resale Prices Act competition between traders became more pronounced although this did not always take the form of price cuts. Trading stamps were increasingly used as a means of increasing trade,[3] but shortly before the Act traders were tempted to reduce the prices of different products often as 'loss leaders'. In order to reduce the chances of prosecution these

---

[1] See C. Fulop, 'Revolution in Retailing', *Hobart Paper No. 9.*

[2] B. S. Yamey, 'Resale Price Maintenance', *Hobart Paper No. 1.*

[3] C. Fulop, 'The Role of Trading Stamps in Retail Competition', *Eaton Paper No. 3.*

firms changed the products used as loss-leaders frequently. In this way the products of any single manufacturer were unlikely to be used consistently as loss-leaders.

7. THE RESALE PRICES ACT 1964

The main provision of this Act, which was passed on the July 16th 1964, was to make all forms of R.P.M. illegal except for those cases in which it is upheld by the Restrictive Practices Court. Firms wishing to continue with their R.P.M. arrangements had to register with the Registrar of Restrictive Practices who in due course referred *groups of agreements* to the Court. (N.B. individual agreements are not referred; the Court is empowered to direct that goods of a *specified class* shall or shall not be allowed to continue their arrangements.) Firms applying for exemption from the ban *are allowed to maintain R.P.M. until their application is heard and a pronouncement made.*

Firms or trade associations had to apply for exemption through any of five 'Gateways':

1. That the quality of goods or their variety would be substantially reduced.
2. That the number of shops in which the goods are sold would be substantially reduced.
3. That prices would be increased in the long run.
4. That goods would be sold under conditions which would cause danger to health.
5. That after-sales service would cease to be provided or would be substantially reduced.

The Second Hurdle: further the Court had to be satisfied that the benefits to the public alleged to accrue from R.P.M. would more than outweigh those benefits deriving from its abolition.

Note the similarity in approach to Part One of the 1956 Legislation in that:

a) All agreements are contrary to the public interest unless proved to be otherwise.
b) Exemption can only be claimed on a few specified counts.
c) Both Acts require parties to clear a double hurdle.

The R.P.M. Register opened on August 16th 1964 for a period of three months. During this period 700 registrations were made covering over 5,000 articles; of these 650 were from suppliers and 50 by trade associations on behalf of their members. More than half of the registrations were made during the last week of the period. Some 23 per cent of the registrations referred to only one good but a few referred to more than 200 goods. It is noteworthy that no claims for exemption were received from motor vehicles and accessories, wallpaper, paints and most sports goods.

When the registration was completed the Registrar classified the goods for two reasons:

    a) So that the public would know which goods could continue with R.P.M. until referred to the R.P. Court.

    b) In order that the goods could be referred to the Court.

Almost 500 classes of goods have been registered and referred to the Court. The Registrar thinks it unlikely that any great number will be contested. This belief is based on his experience from the 1956 Act. During March 1965 nine notes of reference were issued and a further twenty-three by the end of June 1965. These first cases were designed to cover a wide variety of goods in order to guide future cases.[1] By the end of January 1967, 81 notes of reference had been issued covering 322 classes of goods completely and parts of 47 others.

If no defence case is put forward after a reference is made, the Registrar can apply to the Court for a declaration that R.P.M. is prohibited on that class of goods, i.e. the firms can no longer claim exemption from the ban on R.P.M. By January 1968 the Registrar had published eight lists comprising some 500 classes of registered goods; all these classes have been referred to the Court in 157 notices of reference. Already over 300 whole classes of goods and parts of over 50 others are covered by declarations of non-exemption from the ban on R.P.M. The decision not to allow R.P.M. in the case of Chocolate and Sugar Confectionery in July 1967 discouraged many other manufacturers from contesting the proceedings. Obviously many firms and trade associations registered only as a delaying tactic in order to maintain resale prices until the particular class of goods was considered, such firms had no intention of defending their activities.

---

[1] The Registrar stated on February 11th 1965 that the first references would include wines and spirits, footwear, radio and TV sets.

Further developments

In an article in *The Times*[1] Christina Fulop contrasted the way in which some firms publicly abandoned R.P.M., including I.C.I., Dunlop, and Gillette, while other firms did so more discreetly. Where R.P.M. has disappeared supermarkets and discount houses have introduced a wide range of cut-price articles from household appliances and electrical goods where there has been a 16 per cent reduction on average, in the manufacturer's suggested prices, to a 20 per cent reduction in the prices of paints, heat-resistant glassware and batteries. Price reductions for wines and spirits vary considerably. Many manufacturers whose lines have been freed from R.P.M. have refused to supply retailers noted for their aggressive pricing policies. Such firms are then prevented from buying on the best terms and extending to consumers the benefits of their large buying power and low overheads. Mrs. Fulop stated that in a minority of lines it is impossible for enterprising retailers to obtain supplies at all. Such actions contravene the spirit and intention of the 1964 Resale Prices Act and are preventing desirable changes in the structure of distribution taking place.

In November 1966 the Branded Furniture Society announced that it would abandon R.P.M. and not defend it before the Restrictive Practices Court on December 2nd 1966. As a result of this decision it was predicted that furniture prices will fall by between 5-10 per cent.

In January 1967, The Imperial Tobacco Co. decided to abandon R.P.M. and it gave its competitors Gallahers and Carreras two weeks notice of this intention. The news leaked and supermarkets cut prices by as much as 6d. This took Imperial by surprise since they expected a price reduction of 2d. or 3d. Tesco had stocks of fifty million of one manufacturer's brands at the start of the price cutting and within two days it asked for immediate delivery of another hundred and fifty million. Imperial announced at the end of one week that it intended retaining R.P.M.

The first case to be heard by the Court under the 1964 Act, The Chocolate and Confectionery Manufacturers Group, was started on April 10th 1967. The Manufacturers maintained that a wide variety of goods must be available but if R.P.M. was abolished costs would rise and some firms would go out of business thus reducing the variety of good available to the consumer ('Gateway 1'), further trade

---

[1] *The Times* (April 20th 1967, 'How Competition is affecting prices').

margins would be higher and the number of retailers – particularly sweet shops – would fall substantially ('Gateway 2'). The manufacturers stated that the opportunities for price-cutting were small. On July 21st the Court ruled that R.P.M. in confectionery was illegal.

On May 17th 1967 the President of the Board of Trade asked the Monopolies Commission (under Section 5 of the 1965 Monopolies and Mergers Act) to investigate the increasingly widespread practice of recommending standard price lists. The Board was interested in finding out whether this practice was a subtle way of replacing the R.P.M. policies which were being rapidly abandoned. Nearly all manufacturers and suppliers who have abandoned the fixing of prices now recommend retail price levels though shopkeepers and dealers are free to ignore the suggestions if they want to cut prices. The Government wanted to see to what extent competition is restricted or distorted by recommended prices.

Early in 1969 the Commission reported: they found that the effect on the public interest differed between different trades. A comprehensive ban on recommended resale prices would not, in the Commission's view, be justified but the Board of Trade should be empowered to investigate or refer for investigation, the supply of any class of goods and to prohibit the recommendation of resale prices where this was shown to operate against the public interest.

(iii) The Monopolies Commission – Part III of the 1956 Act

Part III of the Act was concerned with monopoly situations that did not come within the scope of the restrictive practices covered by Part I of the Act, which were to be dealt with by the Restrictive Practices Court. The 1956 Act abolished the Monopolies and Restrictive Practices Commission and in its place established a new Monopolies Commission. The maximum number of members was reduced from 25 to 10, and the Commission was no longer able to work in separate groups and consequently no deputy chairman could be appointed. These changes were effected because it was felt that most of its previous responsibilities had been transferred to the Restrictive Practices Court.

The new Monopolies Commission was henceforth to concern itself with unitary monopolies or oligopolies, i.e. to those situations where a single firm or group of related firms is involved in at least one-third of the supply or processing of goods traded in the U.K.; to agreements relating exclusively to the export trade; and to situations where companies responsible for at least one-third of the supply or processing of goods without any *registrable* agreement between them, adopt policies that restrict competition. The Commission was precluded from passing a judgement on any agreement registrable under Part I of the Act.

It was pointed out in the *Times Review of Industry*, March 1964, that the 1953 modifications to the Commission were designed to speed up its work and that these achieved the desired goal. Between 1953–5 seven more reports were completed and useful progress was made on another nine. The 1956 Act put the clock back and placed the Commission in the position it was in during the 1948–53 period when it progressed painfully slowly. It was reasoned in 1956 that since the bulk of the work was being transferred to the Restrictive Practices Court, the Commission would be able to function effectively on its reduced strength and that it would not need the power to work in separate groups. This reasoning was subsequently proved to be wrong: there was plenty of work for the Commission to do. The Commission again progressed slowly as a result of the changes.

Some of the Commission's findings
Between 1956 and 1967 the Commission published 21 reports[1] (including its one and only 'follow-up report', 1958 Follow up on Imported Timber – original report 1953). In this report it was found that nothing had been done to implement the Commission's recommendations despite the assurances given to the Board of Trade, indeed it was found that the restrictions had in fact been extended to include hard and softwoods. As a result an Order was made prohibiting such arrangements. It is recognized that some of the worst restrictions relate to plywoods, but as yet no action has been taken to deal with these. Following the 1960 Report on Chemical Fertilizers the Board of Trade accepted assurances from I.C.I. and Fisons that they would not make unreasonable profits.

The Commission found that the monopoly position of Imperial Tobacco in the Cigarette and Tobacco Industry did not operate

---

[1] In addition the Commission reported on four proposed mergers: B.M.C. and Pressed Steel, The Ross Group and Associated Fisheries, the Dental Merger, and *The Times* and *Sunday Times*.

against the public interest, but that its shareholding in Gallaher did. The Commission therefore recommended that Imperial should dispose of its financial interests in Gallahers. The Board of Trade was satisfied with Imperial's assurance that they would not interfere in the management of Gallaher. In the report on the Supply of Machinery to the Cigarette and Tobacco Industry the Commission found that neither the monopoly position of Molins as the principal supplier of machinery nor the monopsonist (a dominant buyer) position of Imperial Tobacco operated against the public interest.[1]

At the beginning of 1964 the Commission presented its report on the Supply of Wallpaper. This was not a full reference by the Board of Trade but was restricted, limiting the public interest analysis of the Commission to select issues. The reasons for this restricted reference are not known. The Commission recommended that the Wall Paper Manufacturers Ltd., should not in future acquire interests in other firms manufacturing wallpaper without first obtaining permission from the Board of Trade. Furthermore it made recommendations about revising the practice of exclusive dealing and ending R.P.M.[2] However, the Board of Trade accepted assurances from the Company on all these matters. The Monopolies Commission report on the 'solus sites system' of the retail sale of petrol was published in 1965.[3] Monopoly conditions were found in the supply of petrol to retailers and further that agreements between suppliers and retailers operated against the public interest. The recommendations included that 'solus' agreements should only last for five years; that there should be no restrictions on the brands of lubricant, kerosene and anti-freeze that retailers could sell; that agreements should not give suppliers the option to buy the premises of petrol stations; and that no supplier

---

[1] For a case study of the 'Procedure of Inquiry – The Imperial Tobacco Company', see C. K. Rowley, *The British Monopolies Commission*, Appendix 2.

[2] Lucas had a 'Preferential Spares Discount Agreement' with certain distributors which allowed favourable terms in exchange for an agreement to buy spares exclusively from Lucas.

[3] The Solus agreement is a form of exclusive dealing. The petrol company agrees to meet the new garage owner's capital requirements – usually repayable over a period of 14–21 years – in exchange for his agreement to sell their products exclusively. However, the owner is *not* permitted to repay the outstanding capital at an earlier date and consequently the garage is 'tied' to the petrol company.

whose total deliveries exceeded 10m gallons per year should build or acquire more petrol stations while supplies of petrol to company-owned stations exceed 15 per cent of his total. The Board of Trade sought an undertaking from the Petrol Companies concerned that 'tied' garage agreements would be for a maximum period of five years.[1] It was estimated that at the time of the report there were some 30,510 garages operating under 'solus' agreements of which the Shell–B.P., National Benzole–Power groups owned over half.

In this instance all the petrol companies concerned are now renegotiating agreements based on the maximum five-year period recommended by the Monopolies report. The Esso Petroleum Company appealed to the House of Lords against the decision of the Court of Appeal (February 1966) that their agreement with a Worcestershire garage was in 'restraint of trade'.[2] The House of Lords ruled on February 23rd 1967 that the Esso agreement which bound the garage to the petrol company was in '*unreasonable* restraint of trade'. This decision is vital to all the big petrol companies in Britain which operate 'solus' agreements: it means that garages no longer have to accept such long-term agreements which are impossible to break before the stipulated period of the contract is up. This may prevent the petrol companies from embarking on certain aspects of long-term planning now this decision has been reached. After the five-year agreement expires many garages may be in a position to negotiate for renewal of agreements with the company offering the best incentives.[3]

Developments leading to the 1965 Act
After the 1956 Act there was a marked increase in the number of take-overs and mergers that occurred in British Industry. Various reasons have been put forward for this development – the most widely sup-

---

[1] For full details of the Undertakings given by the Suppliers of Petrol see the Annual Report of the Board of Trade for 1966.

[2] Esso Petroleum Co. Ltd. *v.* Harper's Garage (Stourport) Ltd., February 24th, 1966, 2Q.B. 514.

[3] It was announced by the Board of Trade on 4/9/68 that it had received revised undertakings from all suppliers of petrol to retailers in the U.K. effective from 16/8/68. Under these revisions the undertaking limiting the acquisition of company-owned stations has been abandoned; the renewal of leases at tenants' choice should be for minimum periods of three years; and previous undertakings should continue subject only to minor modifications.

ported is that because of the severity in dealing with restrictive agreements by the Restrictive Practices Court some firms sought a more dominant position in the market in order that they would avoid reference by the Registrar to the Restrictive Practices Court. At worst they would be subject to investigation by the Monopolies Commission and from the firms point of view the slight risk involved was justified.[1] Once again discussion and attention centred around the dominant firm. From various quarters there was a demand that the Monopolies Commission should be restored to its 1953 strength.

8. THE 1965 MONOPOLIES AND MERGERS ACT

1. The Commission was enlarged again to a minimum of 4 and a maximum of 25 members. (In March 1969 the President of the Board of Trade appointed seven new members thus bringing the total up from 13 to 20. This followed considerable speculation as to the future of the Commission.) The right for the Commission to work in sub-groups was similarly restored thus allowing it to deal with references more speedily. (i.e. the 1953 position was restored).

2. The Commission was now empowered to investigate (on reference from the Board) restrictive practices and monopoly situations in the *service* industries.

3. The powers of the Board of Trade, to act on the Commission's reports, have been extended: it can now require the publication of price lists, regulate prices, prohibit acquisitions or impose conditions on acquisitions.

4. The Commission may be asked by the Board to investigate mergers to see if they would be against the public interest. The Board may refer cases where a monopoly would be created or strengthened as a result of the merger or where the value of the assets exceeds £5 million. Any mergers must be considered *immediately* by the Board of Trade to avoid delaying the firms unnecessarily; the Commission is required to report on any merger within six months for the same reason. If the merger is thought to be against the public interest the Board may prohibit it 'or dissolve it if it has already taken place). In October 1965 the Board persuaded the Imperial Tobacco Company not to pursue a bid for Smith's Potato Crisps.

In the case of newspapers, it is now illegal for a newspaper to

---

[1] See C. K. Rowley, *The British Monopolies Commission*, ch. 21. Also P. Donaldson, *A Guide to the British Economy*, p. 95.

merge with another paper where the combined average daily circulation exceeds 500,000, without the permission of the Board of Trade. Such permission was granted in 1966 for the transfer of *The Times – Sunday Times* to a new company under the control of the Thomson Organization.

5. Lastly the Board of Trade is empowered to deal with monopolies which operate against any international trade treaty to which the U.K. is a party, e.g. E.F.T.A.

Between 1966–8 the Board of Trade considered nearly 170 significant mergers which satisfied the criteria of the 1965 Monopolies and Mergers Act, of these only eight were referred to the Commission (of which two related to newspapers). The Commission had objected to several proposed mergers on the grounds that they would operate against the public interest: these include those between the Ross Group and Associated Fisheries [though a modified proposal was approved early in 1969): United Drapery Stores and M. Burtons; De la Rue and Rank. In the case of proposed merger between Barclays, Lloyds and Martins the Commission felt that there would be only marginal benefits to the public and voted 6 to 4 against the merger. The Government prohibited this merger in July 1968. Some 130 mergers were examined by the Board of Trade in 1968, of which only two were referred to the Monopolies Commission.

Further developments

In January 1967 the Commission was given its first *general* reference for ten years when it was asked to inquire into restrictive practices in the professions although no definition of a profession was given to them. It was thought that they would inquire into the conditions of entry, fees and commissions, advertising in a wide range of professions including medicine, architecture, surveying and accountancy.[1]

However, in May 1967 it was pointed out that the Commission's terms of reference included the proviso 'that the Commission shall not report on practices expressly authorized by or under any enactment or Royal Charter'. This effectively neutralized what might have been an extremely useful investigation into many of the most restrictive professional practices. Many of these practices have been granted by Royal Charters and Statutes and were therefore outside the Commission's terms of reference. However, in November 1967 the matter was put right; new terms of reference were announced which

---

[1] See the *Sunday Times*, February 5th 1967.

enabled the Commission to examine practices authorized by or under Royal Charter or under Statutes enacted in or before 1955.

In the Commission's Report on the Supply and processing of colour film (April 1966) it was noted that Kodak supplies 70 per cent of the colour film in the U.K. The Commission found that some of the firm's commercial policies operated against the public interest, allowing Kodak's to make an excess profit on colour film, e.g. in 1964 Kodak's colour film business represented only 16½ per cent of its total income yet it yielded 33⅓ per cent of its total net profits. The firm allows excessive retail profit margins too, 30 per cent on sales of Kodak colour film and 33⅓ per cent on processing.

Among its recommendations the Commission suggests the abolition of import duty on colour films in order to make the industry more competitive, and substantial price reductions for Kodak Colour films. In August 1966 Kodak agreed, after negotiations with the Board of Trade to reduce the price of colour film to the retailer by 12½ per cent, but discussions are still continuing on the level of retail profit margins. The Board of Trade is using its powers under the 1965 Act to reduce prices. In its report on Tariffs and Import Duties in September 1967 the Board stated that the removal of the import duty on colour film would not be in the public interest.

In August 1966 the Commission reported on Household Detergents where two firms, Unilever and Proctor and Gamble, dominate the market. It was found that the advertising and promotion policies of these firms operated against the public interest: the Commission therefore included among its recommendations that both companies should cut their sales expenditure by 40 per cent and their prices by about 20 per cent.

The Board of Trade negotiated with the firms involved for eight months during which time the companies maintained that heavy advertising was necessary even for national brands. (The two companies spend £16m per year on advertising.) Gwen Nuttall reported in the *Sunday Times*, April 2nd 1967 that 'throughout the long and difficult negotiations with the Board of Trade the companies have stuck to this line and firmly refused to cut their advertising voluntarily, insisting that only by legislation could the Government make them do so'.

The outcome of the discussions was a compromise. The President of the Board did not attempt to legislate to force the firms to reduce their advertising expenditure. In April 1967 Mr. Douglas Jay announced in the Commons that Unilever and Proctor and Gamble had

51

agreed to market an alternative range of top-quality soap-powders and detergents at a price 20 per cent below the prices of existing products in these categories. These new brands, however, have been advertised far less extensively.[1] Both companies further agreed not to raise the prices of any of the detergents covered by the Monopolies Commission's report for a period of two years.[2]

The President added: 'My examination of this problem has led me to conclude that we know too little about the economic effects of advertising in general and its relationship to competition. I have decided to institute some independent research into this subject and will be consulting industry about its scope. This research will be general and not confined to detergents.' It is expected that the results of this research will be published in 1969.

The Commission's report on Courtauld's in March 1968 sparked off another controversy about the value of the work the Commission was doing. After three years' investigation the Commission found nothing to warrant punitive measures or justify breaking Courtauld's 98 per cent share of Britain's cellulosic market up. It did, however, recommend:

1. that the tariffs which protect Courtauld's from imported rayon should be reduced and

2. that Courtauld's freedom to expand by take-overs should be limited to 25 per cent of any one sector of the clothing or textile industries and a smaller percentage of the wholesale or retail trade.

The second of the Commission's recommendations would have the effect of limiting Courtauld's scope for exploiting its position through tied outlets by restricting the group's activities in the takeover field. Courtaulds subsequently made a bid of £105m for English Calico but bowing to pressure from the Government Courtaulds withdrew the bid on 6th February, 1969. The President of the Board of Trade said that the bid had been withdrawn pending a government review of the whole structure of the Lancashire textile industry. In June 1969 the

---

[1] These brands were marketed for an experimental period of two years: this period expired at the end of May 1969. The Board of Trade is now studying the sales figures of the manufacturers but it appears that the level of sales has been low. *The Times* commented [26/5/69] 'the evident failure of low price detergents can be partially attributed to lack of shelf-display at point of sale, but it seems that the majority of housewives like the ballyhoo which surrounds their washing powders'.

[2] In June 1969 the Board of Trade announced that it was not asking Proctor & Gamble, and Unilever to renew this undertaking.

Board stated 'on balance the best interests of the industry would not be served by a merger between any two of the larger firms in the Lancashire industry at the present time or by a takeover of any of these firms by overseas interests'.

Early in 1968 there were criticisms of inconsistency levied against the Government's policy of promoting industrial mergers through the Industrial Reorganization Corporation and its use of stronger monopolies' legislation. This is a paradoxical situation, but in reality one policy does not exclude the other. The Government obviously wants a more rational industrial structure and in many cases this will mean mergers but it has a duty to ensure that such mergers will not operate against the public interest. *The Times* leader stated 'there need be no conflict between these roles: in many cases industry can benefit from greater size but there must be some organization – the Monopolies Commission – to ensure that the power that goes with size is not abused' (23rd December 1968).

In 1970, with the return of a Conservative Government committed to less intervention in industry, it was no surprise to find policy on industrial structure changing emphasis. The control of monopoly power was to be achieved via the encouragement of competition. To this end, in May 1971, four references were made to the Monopolies Commission: on price leadership and parallel pricing, on electricity and gas connection charges, on the price of breakfast cereals, and on the supply of boot and shoe machinery. Mr. John Davies, the Secretary of State for Trade and Industry, referred these cases under existing legislation but using provisions which had not previously been invoked. In referring gas and electricity connection charges the Minister was also for the first time turning the Commission's attention to the nationalized industries.

A further manifestation of the Government's commitment to the promotion of competition came in the Spring of 1972 with the reference of both the Beecham and Boots bids for Glaxo. The concentration of industry via take-overs had continued into the 1970s (although not at the rate of the boom years of 1968 and 1969 – perhaps as the result of the voluntary efforts of the City through the increasingly effective Take-Over Panel) and many of these mergers had market dominance as their basic motive. It was not perhaps surprising when the Commission ruled against both the proposed mergers, which had been the object of Britain's biggest take-over battle to that date. Despite the Government's attitude, however, take-overs and mergers continued to take place and to do so at an increasing rate, with 1972 as a record year both in terms of number and value.

9. THE RE-STRUCTURING OF GOVERNMENT DEPARTMENTS

On Sunday, 6th October, 1969, Mr. Wilson, the Prime Minister announced a radical re-organization of several Government departments. It has already been pointed out that the Government was promoting mergers through the I.R.C. (which was responsible to the Department of Economic Affairs) and examining the effects of merger through the Monopolies Commission (for the Board of Trade). In the changes that were announced the Ministry of Technology became *in effect* the 'Ministry for Industry' since it took over responsibility for the I.R.C. from the D.E.A., as well as some of the industrial responsibilities from the Board of Trade.

The new styled Board of Trade was to concentrate on overseas trade and export promotion. On October 7th, 1969, the Prime Minister told the N.E.D.C. that a review of the functions and structure of several agencies including the Monopolies Commission and the Registry of Restrictive Trading Agreements would be completed by the end of October. It was subsequently announced that the Department of Employment and Productivity would take over responsibility for both the Monopolies Commission and the Restrictive Trade Practices Court. The I.R.C. was to be responsible to the Ministry of Technology.

A year later, in a White Paper entitled *The Reorganization of Central Government*, the new Conservative Government announced a further rationalization of government departments in an attempt to reduce the influence of government in the economy. All aspects of industrial policy were to be the responsibility of one of the two new 'super-ministries', the Department of Trade and Industry, formed by the merger of the Ministry of Technology and the Board of Trade. As well as the functions of these two departments, the D.T.I. was to take over responsibility for monopolies, mergers, and restrictive practices from the D.E.P. (now renamed the Department of Employment). One consequence of the new Government's approach was the dissolution of the I.R.C. in May 1971.

10. THE 1973 FAIR TRADING ACT

Under this Act monopolies, mergers, restrictive practices, and, specifically, consumer protection were all brought together under one man, the Director-General of the Office of Fair Trading.[1] Although answerable to the Minister, he is responsible for the Monopolies Commission (renamed the Monopolies and Mergers Commission), the Registry of Restrictive Practices, which can now deal with services, and a new Consumer Protection Advisory Committee. Both the private and public sectors can be investigated under the Act, as can local monopolies. The Act also allows the Commission to look at, but not issue orders in relation to, restrictive labour practices on the part of employers or employees. For the first time, as someone other than the Minister, the Director-General has the power to make references, although he can be overruled by the Secretary of State. The Minister retains the power to make references himself and has the sole right to make references concerning mergers, nationalized industries, and other statutory trading bodies. One other detailed change over references is that the qualifying share of the market has been reduced from a third to a quarter.

When the Act was passed it was generally felt that the power given to the Director-General, together with increased staff and greater financial resources, would enable him to keep a closer watch over those aspects of industry's structural policies which were thought to be against the public interest. There were reservations, however. Some commentators felt, for example, that the new legislation should have covered all proposed mergers, particularly in that Ministers, who continued to have the sole right to refer mergers, had shown a particular lack of consistency over references in the past.

Some recent reports
In January 1973 the Monopolies Commission published its report on the supply of asbestos and certain asbestos products. It found that Central Asbestos, with more than one-third of the domestic market in asbestos fibres, and therefore technically a monopoly, was not really in a position to act against the public interest, since most large users of fibres bought their requirements abroad. In the case of asbestos products (e.g. brake linings, clutch facings, and asbestos cement products), the Commission found that, although Turner and Newall, the largest producer with around 40 per cent of the market, was under increasing competitive pressure, it had entered

---

[1]The first Director-General, Mr. John Methven, took up his appointment in December 1973.

into various restrictive agreements with both its competitors and its customers and was thus acting against the public interest. While arguing that the company's monopoly position was not in itself harmful to the public interest, the Commission recommended that the restrictive agreements should cease.

The report on breakfast cereals, published in February 1973, was interesting in that it had been as long ago as 1966 that the Commission had last studied a product (detergent) sold primarily on brand appeal. It will be remembered that the Commission had recommended increased price competition in that case. As for breakfast cereals, the Commission found that Kellogg had 60 per cent of the market, with one brand, *Corn Flakes*, accounting for 30 per cent of all cereals sold in 1971. Kellogg were obviously in a position to determine price levels and this had worked against the public interest in the past (Kellogg's return on capital in the late 1960s had averaged 46 per cent). The Commission recommended that the company's prices and profits should be placed under surveillance in order to safeguard the public interest in the future.

Perhaps the most controversial report published by the Commission appeared in April 1973. The report, on the supply of chlorodiazepoxide and diazepan, dealt with the monopoly prices it was alleged had been charged to the National Health Service (later the Department of Health and Social Security) by Roche Products Limited for tranquillizers patented under the brand names of *Librium* and *Valium*. As soon as they appeared in the early 1960s these drugs were in great demand, as they could be used in place of barbiturates which had proved often dangerous.

In 1967 the Sainsbury Report on the relation between the drug manufacturers and the N.H.S. had argued that prices and profits were sometimes unreasonably high. As a result the drug manufacturers were required to make annual returns to the government detailing their business with the N.H.S. This brought a reduction of prices by most manufacturers, but not by Roche. In the autumn of 1971 the supply of *Librium* and *Valium* was referred to the Monopolies Commission.

The Commission found difficulty in obtaining information from the firm's Swiss parent company, Hoffmann-La Roche, but estimated that the company's return on capital was an excessive 70 per cent. The situation was complicated by the fact that the multinational Hoffman-La Roche was following the standard procedure of transferring costs and revenues from one country to another in order to be seen to make its profits in countries with more favourable tax policies. The Commission estimated that between 1966 and 1972 the profits from the sales of the two drugs were of the order of £24 million, as against the £3 million reported by Roche, and while it recognized that these profits were used primarily to finance research it felt there was a limit to price and profit levels that could be justified in this way.

The Commission recommended that the selling prices of *Valium* and *Librium* should be reduced respectively by 75 and 60 per cent of their 1970 prices and that negotiations should open with a view to the company making a voluntary payment to the D.H.S.S. to compensate for the excessive prices already charged. Roche decided to fight the recommendations and to this end petitioned the Special Orders Committee of the House of Lords. It argued that (i) a cut in price would put them out of business as other governments followed the British lead, (ii) other, U.K. domestic drug companies were making larger profits, and (iii) it was doing no more than British drug companies, who themselves charged higher prices abroad than at home. The Special Orders Committee felt that Roche had grounds for complaint and argued that there should be a House of Lords Select Committee Inquiry into the case. When the House of Lords rejected this suggestion Roche issued a writ on the D.T.I. alleging that the Monopolies Commission Report was contrary to natural justice. It is likely that the legal proceedings will go on until the patents on the two drugs run out and prices inevitably fall as the result of competition from other firms. But by that time, if it can maintain its price levels in the face of pressure in both Britain and Europe (the E.E.C. Commission has begun a comparative study of the prices charged for the drugs in all member countries), Roche is likely to have made as much as possible from its monopoly position.

Some recent references
At the end of 1973 references to the Monopolies Commission included the brick industry and the duplicating equipment industry, where the London Brick Company and Rank-Xerox are dominant in their respective markets, and the bread industry where between them the three largest firms, Rank-Hovis-MacDougall, Associated British Foods, and Spillers-French, account for nearly three-quarters of the market.

New approaches towards monopolies and mergers
In July 1974 two further references – into insulated electric cable and

wire industry and the diazo copying materials industry – were notable for the fact that they were the first made by the Director-General under the powers given him in the Fair Trading Act. In reply to the criticism of lack of consistency over references in the past, the Office of Fair Trading is developing an approach whereby concentrated sectors of industry, wherever they occur, will be systematically screened and their behaviour measured against certain conduct and performance indicators. The above references are interesting in that the findings, when they are published, will be the first to reflect this new approach.

The four conduct indicators are: (i) complaints from trade and consumer sources; (ii) suspected price leadership or parallel pricing; (iii) the ratio of the cost of advertising to the value of sales; and (iv) the degree of merger activity in the industry. The four performance indicators are: (i) the ratio of capital to turnover; (ii) changes in profit margins; (iii) return on capital; and (iv) relative price movements, i.e. in excess of the general level of inflation. It seems that in both the industries referred the return on capital appears to be high enough to indicate the possible existence of barriers to entry into the respective markets.

For mergers too there was a new approach, with a more aggressive policy promised at the end of 1973 by the last Conservative Minister for Trade and Consumer Affairs, Sir Geoffrey Howe. The policy would be more flexible and take account of changing national priorities and the effect of entry into the E.E.C. Throughout, however, the policy would reflect the Conservative Government's belief in competition as a promoter of efficiency.

11. A BRIEF SURVEY OF THE POSITION OF MONOPOLIES AND RESTRICTIVE PRACTICES IN THE EUROPEAN COMMON MARKET

The Common Market provides a strong legal basis for anti-trust operations. The Coal–Steel Treaty (The Paris Treaty 1952) bans agreements or concerted practices in the coal and steel industries which prevent, restrain or distort competition and in particular price-fixing, market-sharing, restriction on output, restriction of technical development and discriminatory supply conditions. The Treaty of Rome of 1958 imposes a similar ban for all industries if such agreements are likely to affect trade between member States. (See Articles 85, 86, and 92.) In practice since most firms within the Community deal within other member countries, it now means that the majority of firms come under the ban. Agreements contributing to better production, distribution, or to technical progress can, however, be authorized.

As regards monopolies, the Coal–Steel Treaty makes all mergers between firms subject to prior authorization by the Coal–Steel Community High Authority, while the Common Market Treaty (Article 86) bans the abuse by one firm or a group of firms of a dominant position in the Common Market (or within a substantial part of it).

A first directive to implement the Treaty of Rome's anti-trust rules was adopted in 1961: it makes the Treaty ban automatically operative, unless authorization had been given by the Commission: it requires the compulsory registration of all agreements; it allows the Commission to impose heavy penalties for infringements of the rules, and it gives important powers of inspection and control to the Commission. Further, the Commission is empowered by the Treaty to prevent firms from abusing any dominant position which they might occupy in the Common Market. The aim of such a policy is to ensure that the benefits which have been gained by the creation of a Common Market and the removal of trade barriers are not cancelled out by restrictive practices between private firms and groups.

Since 1961 decisions by the Common Market Commission and the Court of Justice have begun to lay the basis of a case law whereby specific types of inter company agreements are judged permissible or otherwise. In addition state subsidies to industries are forbidden although special aid for depressed areas and important Community projects are permitted.

In February 1974 the European Parliament decided to establish a Common Market Monopolies Commission, which would give the European Commission control over mergers not just in coal and steel but in all industries. Prior notification would have to be given of any merger that would lead to a group turnover of more than around £400 million a year. Notification, which would affect an estimated ten British companies a year, would involve an automatic three month standstill during which time the proposed merger could not take place. A further nine months would probably be required to investigate the merger, so that firms proposing a merger would have to wait a year in all before they knew if their plans could go ahead. It is likely that this all-embracing European approach would inhibit large scale mergers to a greater extent than the current, more pragmatic, British policy.

12. CONCLUSION

Over the last twenty-five years a great deal has been done to eliminate the evils of monopoly exploitation. The first problem was the inadequacy of the information concerning the types of monopoly and restrictive practice, their extent and their economic effects. Gradually the necessary information was built up from a variety of sources. The 1948 Act established the Monopolies Commission which was fairly successful in its inquiries into the types of monopoly practice and in revealing their extent. The control of monopoly situations was left in the hands of the Board of Trade since the Commission was only empowered to report and recommend action to the Board. Thus the failure to control monopolies adequately in this period, rests largely with the Board of Trade since it usually did little more than to seek assurances from the firms concerned that they would modify their practices. The Commission itself functioned slowly but built up a body of knowledge and experience that aided subsequent legislation.

The 1956 Act adopted a more rigorous approach in dealing with the problems. The Act separated restrictive trading agreements, R.P.M., and Monopolies. It was this Act which assumed restrictive practices to operate against the public interest unless the parties to the agreement could prove otherwise. This was an important departure from the usual English Legal practice. The 1964 R.P.M. Act is very similar in its approach to that of the 1956 Act. Both narrow down the grounds on which firms may seek to justify their arrangements (the so-called 'Gateways') and both have a second hurdle to be jumped (the 'Tailpiece'). Recent legislation continued with this aggressive approach and new powers were given to the Board of Trade under the 1965 Monopolies and Mergers Act. The 1968 Act sought a more flexible approach to the problem but provided for stricter enforcement procedures, and allowed for the exemption of insignificant agreements.

The Fair Trading Act was more than a piece of tidying legislation. The scope of the law has been widened, the Director-General has been given more power than his equivalent predecessors, and more aggressive policies have been pursued, in part as a reflection of the Conservative Government's belief in the efficacy of competition. It is difficult to assess, however, the effects of post-war monopoly legislation in quantitative terms or to say how much more efficient British industry has become as a direct result of this legislation. Apparently many undesirable practices have been curtailed but it appears they re-appear in a different guise. Monopoly itself is not harmful, indeed as we have seen earlier, a monopolistic structure may be demanded for an industry in order, for example, to gain the full advantages of the economies of scale. However the Government must ensure that the monopoly does not operate against the public interest.

The phrase 'the public interest' is in a sense the key to the whole problem because it is so difficult to define what the term means. No Act covering monopoly (or for that matter Nationalization) has attempted a definition of 'the public interest'. Consequently it is left to those concerned to interpret the meaning for each particular case under consideration.

It must be realized that although successive British Governments have sought to make British industry more competitive, a state of perfect competition cannot in fact ever be achieved. At best therefore the Government can only hope to remove the most distasteful mono-polistic practices; other market imperfections will still exist. It must be remembered that *competition, too, can be wasteful* and to cause a monopoly to be replaced by oligopoly does not mean that the com-munity will necessarily gain. The degree to which governments seek to control monopoly and restrictive practices is dependent on the political climate. Here is a case where the law of diminishing marginal returns may apply: considerable government time may well produce only a minor improvement in legislation. It is advisable to consider the opportunity cost of introducing minor amendments into a Parli-amentary timetable which is already overcrowded. Furthermore shrewd company lawyers are quick to spot loopholes in the legislation and companies are not slow to exploit such weaknesses.

SELECTED BIBLIOGRAPHY

Standard Texts.
  G. C. Allen, *Monopoly and Restrictive Practices.*
  C. Brock, *The Control of Restrictive Practices Since 1956.*
  P. Guenault and J. Jackson, *The Control of Monopoly in the U.K.*
  C. K. Rowley, *The British Monopolies Commission.*
Articles.
  'British Monopoly Legislation', *Midland Bank Review*, Nov. 1965.
  'The Control of Monopoly', *Lloyds Bank Review*, Oct. 1956.
Official.

Reports of the Registrar of Restrictive Trading Agreements.
(See February 1967 for the Registrar's survey of his progress over the period 1957–67.) Published by the Stationery Office each February.

General.

A. Beacham and L. Williams, *The Economics of Industrial Organization*, ch. 4.

J. W. Grove, *Government and Industry in Britain*, ch. 7.

C. Fulop, 'The Role of Trading Stamps in Retail Competition', *Eaton Papers*.

G. Hutton (Ed.), *Source Book on Restrictive Practices in Britain* (Institute of Economic Affairs).

'Which way Monopoly Policy?' G. Polanyi I.E.A. Research Monograph 30.

Midland Bank Review – 'Government and Business' section provides useful information on current developments.

SELECTED QUESTIONS

1. Outline the methods employed in the U.K. to control monopolies and restrictive practices and consider their adequacy. (*London*)

2. In what circumstances might it be desirable to control monopolistic practices and how might this be done? (*London*)

3. Explain in general terms the workings of the 1956 Restrictive Trade Practices Act. (*London*)

4. Consider the case for extending the scope of the monopolistic and restrictive trade practices legislation to cover all the markets for goods and factor services. (*Cambridge*)

5. Discuss with practical examples possible methods of preventing the 'evils of monopoly'. (*Cambridge*)

6. In what circumstances, if any, should the maintenance of resale prices by manufacturers be permitted? (*Cambridge*)

7. How may monopolies be controlled? (*Chartered Insurance Institute*)

8. Discuss the nature and effectiveness of the steps taken in Great Britain to control monopolies. (*Chartered Insurance Institute*)

9. Should legislation concerning monopoly focus attention more on the concentration of monopoly power or more on monopolistic trade practices? (*Cambridge*)

PART 3
CASE STUDIES

INTRODUCTION

The industrial and business history of the twentieth century is characterized by the growth of business units. There has been an increase in the number of firms and there has been a growth in the size of firms. More and more industries have come to be dominated by a small number of large firms in such a way that these firms have a powerful influence on the market. This ability of a firm significantly to influence its market is a simple definition of monopoly power. The Monopolies Commission is empowered to investigate when the firm controls more than one-third of the supply of a particular commodity. These powers have already been exercised in several industries, e.g. Sewing Cotton (J. & P. Coats), Oxygen (British Oxygen Company), Electrical Supplies to Car Industry (J. Lucas), Tobacco (Imperial Tobacco Industry), Films (Kodak), Wallpaper (Sandersons).

Many reasons have been advanced for the growth in the size of firms, and for the emergence of monopoly power, and some of these are discussed below along with the advantages and disadvantages of this growth. In general, there is much to be commended in the growth in size of firms which is in the public interest, while the build-up of monopoly power is seldom to the advantage of the consumer. However, it is often difficult to achieve the advantages of the growth in size without the risk of a build-up of monopoly power. The growth of the Big Four Motor Manufacturers has given them over 98 per cent of the market. The three biggest man-made fibre producers have over 90 per cent of the market. The British Oxygen Company controls 98 per cent of the supply of oxygen; while the two biggest tobacco manufacturers are responsible for over 90 per cent of the output of that industry. Many other examples could be cited where the growth of a few major firms has given them control of a large share of the market. These firms are then in the position to use the weapons of a monopolist.

1. THE TOBACCO INDUSTRY

The process of growth to monopoly power can be well illustrated from the history of the tobacco industry during this century. In 1900 there were about five hundred tobacco manufacturers in the United Kingdom of which W.D. and H.O. Wills was by far the largest. The process of growth had already begun by this date and several of the manufacturers had acquired wholesale or retail outlets, and some had merged with other manufacturers. The combination of firms into multiple concerns had also begun in the retail sector of the industry, and although there were some 300,000 independent retailers, there were already some large multiple concerns like Salmon and Gluckstein.

The growing intensity of competition in an industry has often caused producers to make defensive reactions, which lead to a reduction in the amount of competition, and the genesis of a movement towards monopolistic practices in the industry. Such was the case in tobacco. In 1901 the American Tobacco Co., which controlled a large part of the tobacco trade of the United States, began a campaign which aimed at capturing the English and European trade. They already had depots in the U.K., and they bought up a leading tobacco manufacturer, Ogdens, to provide further facilities for their campaign. Thirteen leading British manufacturers met to decide how to deal with his threat. The outcome of the meeting was the amalgamation of these firms into a company strong enough to meet the American competition. In December 1901 the Imperial Tobacco Company was formed.

The new company adopted various methods to meet the Americans' aggressive sales methods. They continued the process of growth of the company and secured more retail outlets for their products by gaining control of Salmon and Gluckstein. In this they were influenced by the fear that the Americans would buy up this multiple concern. This motive to growth – the fear that a rival firm will expand in the market by combining with another firm – occurs frequently in industrial history. Imperial then introduced a bonus scheme, for profit sharing with trade customers. This market discrimination was unpopular with wholesalers and distributors, and it led to the formation of the Wholesale Tobacco Protection Association. A powerful counter to the American threat was the investigation, which Imperial initiated, of the possibility of their entry into the American market. Again the threat of more intensive competition resulted in an extension of dominant power.

The agreement between the American Tobacco Co. and the Imperial Tobacco Co., which ended the American campaign in the U.K., provided that there should be no competition between the firms in their home markets; that the British-American Tobacco Co. Ltd (B.A.T.), of which the Americans owned two-thirds and Imperial one-third of the share capital, should control the exports of the two companies; and that Imperial's share of the home market should be increased by the transfer of control of Ogden's to Imperial. By 1903 Imperial controlled 47 per cent of the tobacco trade. Their main competitors were Gallaher, Godfrey Phillips, Carreras, J. Wix, and C.W.S.

Imperial already had a powerful monopolistic influence on the market, and as the number of independent tobacco manufacturers steadily declined after 1914, Imperial's share of the market increased – 57 per cent in 1910, 62 per cent in 1915, 73 per cent in 1920. Vertical and horizontal integration of units within the company structure enabled Imperial to increase in power and efficiency. Sources of raw materials were safeguarded (*vertical integration*) by the establishment of leaf-buying organizations in U.S. and Africa. The table below shows how the eighteen firms which made up the Imperial Tobacco Company have been merged (*horizontal integration*) until today there are only four separate units.

	1930	1950	1970
W. D. & H. O. Wills Stephen Mitchell & Son F. & J. Smith ⎱ 1918 Dr. J. MacDonald ⎰	Wills Mitchell ⎱ 1932 Smith ⎰	Wills Mitchell ⎱ 1957	Wills
John Player & Son	Player	Player	Player
Ogden William Clark & Son ⎱ 1923 Hignett Bros. Hignett Tobacco Co. ⎱ 1902 The Richmond Cavendish Co.	Ogden ⎱ 1930 Hignett ⎰	Ogden	⎱ '59 Ogden
W. & F. Faulkner Adkin & Sons W. & T. Davies	Faulkner ⎱ 1946 Adkin ⎰ Davies	Faulkner ⎱ '54 Davies ⎰	

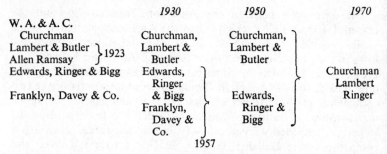

	1930	1950	1970

W. A. & A. C.
Churchman
Lambert & Butler ⎫
Allen Ramsay ⎭ 1923

Churchman,
Lambert &
Butler

Churchman,
Lambert &
Butler

Edwards, Ringer & Bigg

Edwards,
Ringer
& Bigg

Franklyn, Davey & Co.

Franklyn,
Davey &
Co.

Edwards,
Ringer &
Bigg

Churchman
Lambert
Ringer

1957

Government interest in the growth of monopolies had some impact on the Imperial Tobacco Company in the 1910's. First, the United States Anti-trust Laws broke up the American Tobacco Co. into a number of separate firms who became free to export to the U.K. and thus ending the I–A agreement in 1911; and then in 1919 a sub-committee of the Standing Committee on Trusts, under the chairmanship of Sidney Webb was set up to investigate Imperial. The report noted Imperial's dominant position in the trade, but concluded that it was not using its power against the interests of the consumer.

Imperial's share of the market continued to grow in the 1920's when they acquired the Ardath Tobacco Co. Ltd. (jointly with B.A.T.), and a controlling interest in the multiple retail concern, Finlay & Co. Ltd. Their position within the industry was strengthened when the acquisition of a large stake in Molins Machine Co. Ltd. gave them a powerful influence in an important supplier of tobacco machinery. The bargaining position of the firm was thus enhanced by a policy of integration and self-sufficiency.

The war period brought a suspension of normal trading conditions, but in 1947 Imperial's share of the market was the same as in 1934. The post-war situation was complicated by the Dollar Crisis. With every effort being made to reduce imports from the dollar area, Imperial gave an undertaking to keep the proportion of tobacco from this area in the cigarettes down to 61 per cent. Gallahers seized the chance for an effective sales drive winning customers for their 'All-Virginian' Senior Service and Park Drive cigarettes.

One of the reasons for horizontal integration, the combination between firms operating the same processes, is to make further economies of scale possible. Another reason is to reduce the number of firms competing in the market, or to gain control of the production of a particular product. By 1932 Gallaher had become the fourth largest tobacco manufacturer, and in that year Imperial quietly acquired a controlling interest in the company, which it retained until 1946. Little attempt was made to interfere with its policy. The acquisition has been described as a defensive move. The American Tobacco Co. had recently acquired J. Wix and had been contemplating obtaining control of Gallahers. The process of amalgamation continued when Gallahers acquired E. Robinson & Son Ltd. and its associated firms, and J. A. Pattreioux (Senior Service) in 1937.

The Walters episode is another example of the way a monopolist reduces competition. The introduction of Imperial Preference – imports from countries in the British Empire were liable to a lower rate of duty than similar imports from countries outside the Empire – as a result of the Ottawa Agreement of 1932 made the use of leaf from Canada, Rhodesia and other Empire countries much more attractive. In 1934 a company which was new to the trade, Walters Tobacco Co. Ltd. took advantage of the situation to produce a cigarette of empire tobacco to compete in the small cigarette range at the same price but larger than rival makes. This competition through quantity was immediately successful and unwelcome to the established small cigarette manufacturers. Imperial, Carreras, Gallaher, and Godfrey-Phillips decided to push the Walters' 'Empire Tenner' (medium Navy Cut) out of the market. Imperial was encouraged by other manufacturers to produce an Empire brand cigarette to compete with Walters. This Churchman's Tenner achieved substantial sales and pressure was put on Walters at first not to try to increase sales, but to bring both cigarettes on to 'a reasonably profitable basis', then not to bring out similar brands, and finally to sell out completely to Imperial. On January 1st 1938 Imperial acquired Walters and, despite promises to their competitors, continued the 'Empire Tenner' line profitably until rising costs intervened in the 1940's.

Imperial did not encourage price competition either among their own distributors and retailers or among the tobacco manufacturers. In fact every effort was made to prevent price cutting. In spite of this in the early 1930's there were some members of the trade prepared to risk the 'Stop List' which some tobacco manufacturers applied. This device has been a well-used weapon of the monopolist in a variety of trades. Any member of the trade found cutting prices or breaking agreements in any other way were unable to secure supplies from the manufacturers.

Imperial was not a member of the Tobacco Trade Advisory Committee formed in 1926 to combat price fixing, but in a further effort to apply Resale Price Maintenance – insistence by the manufacturer on a fixed price for the sale of his product – Imperial helped to form the Tobacco Trade Association in 1931. Other members of the Association came from the Council of Tobacco Manufacturers and the two distributors organizations. The Association was primarily concerned with limiting price competition at the retail end, and in 1934 dealers were obliged to enter into agreements binding them not to sell below the prescribed selling price, and making them liable to damages if they did. This 'Damages Agreement' promoted by Imperial is an example of the use of a manufacturer's monopoly power over the retailer. Eight hundred retailers signed Imperial's 'Agreement' and by 1939 there was very little price cutting. (See Note below.)

The dominant position of Imperial and its share of the market continued to increase throughout the 1920's until in 1928 some 80 per cent of the cigarette trade was in its hands. But competition remained a real factor influencing Imperial's market policy. Other firms attempted to enlarge their share of the market. Carreras bought John Sinclair Ltd., a manufacturing business with wholesale and retail branches. But the biggest threat to Imperial's position was the introduction of coupon schemes by Wix and Godfrey-Phillips. Where price competition has been restricted or prevented by an oligopolistic market situation, other forms of competition often emerge. Competition through advertising had already emerged in the industry, and now competition through gift coupons and trading stamps spread to the British tobacco industry from the United States.

Imperial were against the introduction of this type of competition, and gave evidence to an independent committee set up to examine the use of gift coupons and trading stamps, claiming that they caused a deterioration in the quality of the product, and competition through quality should be encouraged. By 1933 Imperial's share of the market had declined to 65 per cent, and they were forced to meet this successful competition by introducing their own coupon cigarettes 'Four Aces' through Wills. Ardath had been in the coupon business since 1927. When a Committee set up by the Board of Trade did not recommend prohibiting coupons Imperial persuaded Gallaher, Carreras, Godfrey-Phillips, Wix, and the International Tobacco Company to end their coupons. This, the Martin Agreement, gave certain safeguards to the smaller companies and coupon competition ended on December 31st 1933. Imperial's share of the market rose to 79 per cent in 1934.

The issue of cigarette cards had proved an effective way of attracting customers in the 1930's and this type of competition was not affected by the Martin Agreement. They came to an end as part of wartime economies. In the 1950's the Government attitude towards monopoly and restrictive practices was beginning to harden and in 1956 the Restrictive Trade Practices Act was passed. Sensing the change of attitude Imperial had laid in a stock of cards in anticipation of this type of competition. They were anxious not to start the battle but to be prepared. In the event when the Tobacco Trade Association, and the arrangements for collective price maintenance, was wound up, and the Martin Agreement lapsed, competition through cigarette cards did not break out. It was a coupon-gift scheme introduced by Wix & Co., now owned by American Tobacco, which Imperial had to face. To persuade other firms not to follow the example Imperial considered a compensation scheme, which amounted to a payment to refrain from competition. But the sale of coupon cigarettes has continued to expand and Imperial's share of the market has been eroded a little. In 1967 Imperial and Gallaher announced that gift coupons could be converted into cash. Cash convertibility is another stage in the attempt of tobacco manufacturers to improve their market position at the expense of their rivals. Gallaher has accepted this new form of competition reluctantly and Carreras want new talks on framing a voluntary code for restricting gift coupon brands. The oligopolistic position of these manufacturers might be further threatened by curbs on advertising (as with the prohibition of TV advertising) in the future.

	% 1954	% 1959	% 1967
Imperial	75·4	63·4	63
Gallaher	11·2	29·3	30
Ardath, Carreras, G/P, Rothman and J. Wix	11·9	6·6	7
Others	1·0	0·7	
Value:	£777 million	£933 million	

A further attempt by Imperial to limit competition and to gain preferential treatment in retailing tobacco products occurred when they secured special arrangements with Savoy Hotels that only Imperial's brands of Virginian cigarettes should be sold in their hotels (plus one other brand). Lyons agreed to limit the sales of makes other than Imperials, and G.W.R. were persuaded to install only British

Automatic Cigarette Machines on their stations. Imperial lent British Automatic the vending machines. (For R.P.M. and Tobacco see p. 87.)

The Imperial Tobacco Company have suggested that their monopoly position is tempered by the high degree of autonomy of the firms which make up the company. Each branch is 'a separate trading entity which maintains its own sales force and customers' accounts, and controls its own administration of manufacturing and selling activities. The branch only refers to the Executive Committee items of major capital expenditure, introduction of new brands, price changes and advertising grants. A strongly competitive spirit between the constituent branches is essential to the company's well-being'. (Report to Monopolies Commission.)

The table outlining the percentage share of Imperial's total cigarette and tobacco sales in this century illustrates the real nature of competition between constituent firms, although the picture is affected by several mergers:

Cigarettes	1905 %	1920 %	1938 %	1956 %	1959 %
Wills	24·5	43·1	40·4	40·5	39·7
Player	4·6	17·3	36·6	47·8	47·0
Tobacco					
Wills	8·1	4·3	1·8	2·1	3·5
Player	3·2	2·9	4·3	1·9	2·4
Ogden	15·3	9·4	4·1	3·0	3·8
Ringer	3·4	1·3	0·7	1·8	2·0

The aim of the company is 'to give in all its brands the best possible value for money to the consuming public consistent with both a reasonable margin of profit to the company and a reasonable margin to the distributive trade'. In a competitive situation profit margins can be maintained by competition through weight.

Although the number of tobacco manufacturers has declined from over five hundred at the beginning of the century to twenty-four, there are still over two hundred brands of cigarettes and over four hundred brands of tobacco. But the Monopolies Commission Report in agreeing that there is some measure of competition in the industry, point to several areas of monopoly power. There are six main conclusions:

1. There is reasonable freedom of entry into the market especially for the small manufacturer concentrating on a single brand.
2. Imperial's rate of profit is not contrary to the public interest.

3. There is no reason to criticize the self-sufficiency of Imperial.
4. The Bonus Agreement by which the display facilities by retailers for brands other than Imperials are limited may have contributed to Imperial's dominant position.
5. Gallaher's increased share of the market has produced a more real competitive situation which did not exist before, especially when Imperial had a share in Gallaher's profits.
6. Internal competition is a poor substitute for real competition.

This case study outlines the development of a company into a dominant position in a market. The methods used to achieve and maintain this position have been pointed out, and the use of the monopoly power as examined by the Monopolies Commission has been discussed.

Note 1.   Imperial point out that the 'Damages Agreements' were introduced by the T.T.A. They had to be signed by traders who had indulged in price cutting in the past but had decided to conform in future to the conditions of T.T.A. agreements.

Note 2.   Imperial is not of course a monopolist in the absolute sense and is indeed at the present time exposed to vigorous and effective competition'. (M.C.R.)

2. THE SUPPLY OF INDUSTRIAL GASES

The second case study outlines the development and maintenance of a monopoly position by a firm supplying oxygen and other industrial gases, the British Oxygen Company Ltd. Monopoly Legislation concerns firms which control more than one-third of the supply of a commodity in the U.K. The B.O.C. Group until recently produced more than 98 per cent of oxygen supplied in Britain. The position has been eroded by Air Products. Many of the weapons used by the monopolist in the first case study also appear in this industry. These aim at suppressing and restricting competition. This study also illustrates the use of other methods for strengthening the monopolist's position.

In the closing years of the nineteenth century the policy which was to lead to complete dominance of the market got underway when in 1896 the Birmingham Oxygen Co. Ltd. and the Manchester Oxygen Co. were licensed by Brins (B.O.C.) by this process and the Company was able to extend its activities into new markets in parts of the country it had not previously supplied.

At this stage the industry was in its infancy and methods of production in the world were varied and often inefficient. Most of the early improvements in the production of oxygen came to this country from abroad – Germany, France and U.S.A. – under licence. This method of increasing the efficiency of production was used by B.O.C. The Air liquifaction process improved by Hampson was financed by Brins (B.O.C.) and a patent acquired. By buying the patent rights other firms were prevented from using these methods. B.O.C. also acquired other companies in Britain in order to make use of the particular production techniques used by these companies. In 1906 the Linde British Refrigeration Co. Ltd. and in 1909 the British Liquid Air Ltd. went out of competition with the B.O.C. group. The process of growth continued with the acquisition of the Scotch & Irish Oxygen Co. Ltd. in 1909 and the Knowles Oxygen Co. Ltd. in 1914.

The justification of all these acquisitions on the grounds of promoting efficiency, reducing costs, and enabling gases to be produced and distributed over a wide area at a fair price seems more acceptable in these early instances. Later in B.O.C.'s history they acquired firms which produced oxygen chiefly for their own use and marketed only what was in excess of their needs. The Plymouth Oxygen Co. Ltd. sold their oxygen plant and interests to B.O.C. in 1928, and market pressures forced Edgar J. Rees Ltd. to follow suit in 1934 and Thos. W. Ward Ltd. in 1944. Over the same period B.O.C. persuaded several other firms, which produced oxygen solely for their own use, to close down their plants or to sell them to B.O.C. The Caledon Shipbuilding & Engineering Co. Ltd. and G. A. Harvey & Co. (London) Ltd. came to such an agreement with B.O.C. These closures, the Company claim, occurred because the air separation process is highly sensitive to scale and B.O.C. could offer oxygen to the 'make-it-yourself' user at much more favourable rates.

The process of growth to monopoly power which restricted competition most seriously was that which gave B.O.C. almost complete control over the supply of oxygen plant. Some of the acquisitions mentioned above resulted in firms which had previously produced their own oxygen becoming dependent on B.O.C. During the same period two of the main alternative suppliers of oxygen plant were taken over by B.O.C.; Liquid Air Ltd. in 1929, and Oxhycarbon Ltd. in 1934. After this time the only effective competition in the supply of oxygen plant came from foreign firms, and the home market was powerfully controlled by B.O.C. Although the Company claim that it was open to any other firm to start up in competition by this time 1929–34 as the dominant patents had long lapsed.

Meanwhile the normal process of amalgamation had continued and between 1930 and 1934 Allen-Liversidge Ltd., Oxygen Industries Ltd. and British Industrial Gases Ltd. joined the group.

It has been argued that several firms asked to be taken over as it became more and more costly to carry out the renewal and modernization of plant essential to efficient production. Amalgamation enabled the group to avoid duplication of works capacity, transport, plants, management and offices. Works could be placed to cover practically all industrial areas and ensure prompt economic delivery. Monopoly was the accident of a policy designed to increase efficiency.

The Saturn Industrial Gases Co. Ltd. is the only other producer of any size in the industry and is responsible for just over 1 per cent of the total output. In 1936 it was a private company called the Saturn Oxygen Co. Ltd., and it began a policy of expansion by acquiring patent rights from certain American companies including the Gas Industries Company of Pittsburg. Saturn concentrated with some success on supplying oxygen for the industries of North-East England, an area not well covered by B.O.C.'s production network. In 1937 it began production at Thornaby-on-Tees and in 1939 it extended its activities to Sunderland. The clash with B.O.C. came when Saturn attempted to break into the Scottish market by starting production in Glasgow in 1938. To combat the initial success of Saturn's venture B.O.C. made use of a company not then known to be a subsidiary of British Oxygen – Industrial Gases (Scotland) Ltd. This firm was instructed to offer the product for sale in the Glasgow market at a lower price than Saturn could supply oxygen. This method of competition designed eventually to strengthen the position of the monopolist is based on local and selective reductions in prices instead of providing benefits to all consumers. This use of fighting companies, like Industrial Gases (Scotland) Ltd., or Oxhycarbon Ltd. and British Industrial Gases Ltd. in other instances, is not in the long-term public interest because the monopolist is supplying the commodity at an artificially low price in order to drive out its competitor. In the long run the consumer will have to depend entirely on the supply of the monopolist.

Saturn were forced to leave the Glasgow market and, in keeping with their policy of taking over all other producers of oxygen primarily to extend or preserve its monopoly, B.O.C. began talks with Saturn aimed at Saturn joining the group. But these talks of 1941–2, and the later discussions of 1949 came to nothing. In 1953 Saturn took over the activities of several subsidiaries and by 1954 the supply of oxygen was distributed as follows:

Supplier	*1,000 cu. ft.*	%
B.O.C. Group	5,501,701	98·5
Saturn	77,304	1·4
*Others	4,424	0·1
Total	5,583,430	100

Chiefly Lea & Son (Runcorn) Ltd.

B.O.C. Group

Subsidiaries	*Associated Co.*
British Industrial Gases	Anglia Industrial Gases
British Oxygen Chemicals	B.O.C. Airco Cryogenic Plant
Edwards High Vacuum	B.O. Linde
Muvex	Methane Gas Engineering
Muvex Welding	Northern Liquid Petroleum
	Seaflame Conversion

The main customers of these suppliers were:

Steel Industry	35%
Car Manufacturers	20%
Scrap, Garages	20%
General Engineers	12%
Shipbuilders	10%
Medical	2%

The most recent of B.O.C.'s acquisitions was Edwards High Vacuum International Ltd. which specializes in design and manufacture of equipment.

The possible dangers in the control by one supplier of so large a proportion of the market for oxygen have been pointed out in the Monopolies Commission Report. B.O.C. is able to fix prices and, with a knowledge of the costs it will incur in producing a given output, it can determine the profits it will make. The profits might well be excessive, and if so the consumer will suffer. B.O.C. has little to fear from competitors and it enjoys the monopolist's advantage of certainty of future sales. The cost of oxygen represents a very small part of the total costs of the firms it supplies, e.g. a steel mill, and so it is relatively easy for B.O.C. to pass an increase in costs in higher prices to consumers. The company can make an easy assessment of the market and so the element of risk (for which profit is a reward) is small. The cost of borrowing to meet investment programmes should be relatively low and there is little need for ploughing back profits when the capital can be raised by the issue of debentures. An analysis of B.O.C.'s prices and profits over a period of years suggested to the Commission that both were unjustifiably high and operated against the public interest. In a more competitive situation prices and profits are more likely to be forced down to a level more suited to the particular conditions of the industry.

The monopolist should not take advantage of his power to discriminate 'either between individual consumers or between classes of consumers in similar circumstances' (M.C.R.). It is difficult to equate the secrecy over the prices of B.O.C.'s products with the aim of 'perfect knowledge' in the market.

The bargaining advantage in the industry obviously lies with the supplier of oxygen and not the consumer, and it seems unreasonable that the supplier should use this advantage to limit the right of the customer to buy where he pleases by insisting on exclusivity terms in contracts, i.e. firms that B.O.C. supply must not buy part of their supply from elsewhere.

An important argument in favour of a policy of growth towards larger scale of production is that it enables the firm to undertake research and development to meet the future requirements of customers and to enable the country to compete effectively with similar industries in other countries. If B.O.C. rely for major innovations on improvements introduced from abroad, it is not clear that they are fulfilling this function adequately.

However, there is no evidence that B.O.C. operates less efficiently than would be the case if there were more competition. If the monopoly does not operate with the greatest possible efficiency the public suffers because resources are wasted or because services are not adequate. B.O.C.'s technical services are comprehensive although the cost could be more fairly distributed to customers, thus avoiding the charge of discrimination which is often laid against monopolists. There is always a temptation to favour the large customer, and while this may be justified where economies of scale enable lower rates to be quoted, it is less reasonable when the lower rates are the result of the greater bargaining power of the large customer.

The State has created public monopolies, the nationalized industries, in some cases where the service to consumers is an essential one. It has been argued that the essential nature of the service provided by B.O.C. justifies the control of such a large share of the market. If the supply of oxygen fails the steel industry, shipbuilding, hospitals and others will be seriously affected. The diversification of plant and processes of production only open to a large firm is necessary to safeguard customers from breakdown.

In this case study of the supply of oxygen it can be seen that there are substantial economies of scale to support the need for a firm employing large-scale techniques. But there are considerable disadvantages in the control of almost the whole market by a single group. These disadvantages are accentuated when the group is not prepared to maintain its position simply by its advantages in the scale of production, experience and techniques, but adopts an active policy of suppressing and restricting competition, depriving the public of alternative sources of supply and service. Control over the provision of plant and machinery for the production of the commodity, which the monopolist itself produces, had become more damaging now that new style tonnage equipment enables large users of oxygen to meet their own needs efficiently.

In reply to the charge of monopoly control B.O.C. have pointed out that the position has changed somewhat since the Monopolies Commission Report. Air Products Ltd., the U.K. subsidiary of a large U.S. concern, which entered the British gases (not just oxygen) market in 1957 and now claims about 20 per cent of that market. The international giants in the industrial gas business are Union Carbide, with Airco, L'Air Liquide and B.O.C. The emergence of the Japanese industrial gas companies as major contenders for plant orders in world markets has given impetus to the trend away from the understanding that 'no one bid seriously in anyone else's backyard'. They are active not only in the traditional cylinder market but also in the supply of 'tonnage' oxygen to the steel and chemical industries. B.O.C. stress the fact that they produce a number of products apart from oxygen – nitrogen and argon, helium, neon, krypton and xenon, and supply fuel gases such as acetylene, liquified petroleum gases and liquified natural gas. They claim that in these markets and in the manufacture of industrial equipment there is 'severe British and International competition'.

3. THE MOTOR INDUSTRY

The third case study deals with the historical development of competition in the motor industry which has culminated in a series of recent mergers consolidating production in the hands of four big producers. Prof. J. K. Galbraith has argued that the power of the large corporation is so great that it should be exercised through the State, which will not operate the monopoly powers in the interests of the producer, but with 'social purpose'. But recent mergers have received the direct support of the Government through the work of the Industrial Reorganization Corporation, which aims at encouraging business units of a size better suited to efficient production and international competition.

In the first case study we examined a market situation where there was a dominant firm exercising monopoly power, but where the existence of competition imposed some checks and safeguards on the use of this power. In the second case these checks and safeguards on the actions of the dominant firm were almost entirely missing. In the motor industry the market situation is again different. Although British Leyland Motor Holdings controls over one-third of the total supply (the Monopolies Commission definition of a monopoly) its major rivals are not significantly weaker in their position in the market. It is essentially an oligopolistic situation where the decisions of any one of the major producers is likely to affect and be affected by the decisions of its rivals. The story of how the present pattern of four major producers, B.L.M.C., Ford, Vauxhall and Rootes, and a decreasing number of small independent producers, came to emerge, is outlined in succeeding paragraphs. The picture in 1968 was:

	Cars ,000	%	Commercial Vehicles ,000	%
Total Production	1,816	100	409	100
The Big 4 (Br. Leyland, Ford, Rootes, Vauxhall)	1,806	99	400	98
British Leyland	819	45	169	41

See Appendix 1.

After the First World War two firms emerged to dominate the industry in the 1920's. Morris and Austin accounted for nearly 60 per cent of the total output, and with Singer for three-quarters of total trade. Inability to keep up with the technical advances and improved methods of production of the rapidly expanding major firms resulted in many small producers withdrawing from production or merging with larger firms. A fundamental factor, determining which firms are able to expand their share of the market, is the economies of scale which result from an increase in the scale of production. The advantage to be gained from this expansion is chiefly in the form of lower unit costs of production, and it is because efforts to achieve the lowest possible costs is one of the main forms of competition that economies of scale are such a fundamental factor. In the 20's the large firms were introducing the early mass production techniques made possible by the long-production runs of highly successful models. The technical economies resulting from these steps brought the large firms cumulative advantages which opened a gap between the few large mass producers and a larger number of specialists. The market was not large enough for many firms to promote the expansion programmes which brought efficient, low-cost production. But the difference in production methods was not yet big enough to make impossible the growth of a small independent firm into an effective competitor.

The first firm to break into the 'first division' of car producers was Ford. With the advantage of strong backing from Ford of America, particularly enjoying the fruits of American research, this company was eventually able to produce a product to compete through quality rather than cheapness, with the products of Austin and Morris. But Ford's campaign to capture a larger share of the market had begun with a slashing reduction of the price of the Ford 8 to meet the successful run of the Morris 8. The success of this move depended on a large increase in demand for Ford, and no retaliation from Morris. The increase in demand making possible economies from increased production was achieved, but with little increase in trading profits.

In the previous case studies we have seen the methods used by the dominant producers to gain advantage over their competitors, and to increase their share of the market. Often these methods resulted in the restriction or suppression of competition. This is not the pattern of market behaviour in the motor-car industry. Although the manufacturers are interested in maximization of profits they have taken the long-term view, and have been not much interested in short-term success over their rivals. The methods of a highly competitive market with a large number of participants have not featured prominently in the motor trade. In the 1930's there was very little short-period price competition, and changes in car prices were usually the result of increases in the prices of materials or other costs.

Price leadership is often a feature of a market with a small number of large firms, so that the only price changes in this imperfect oligopolistic market occur when the other firms follow the initiative of the price leader. In this way price competition is limited and is largely dictated by the leader. The position has sometimes been made more certain for the oligopolists by price agreements, by which parties undertake to inform the others of any projected price change.

The oligopoly in the car industry has undoubtedly been largely responsible for the short-run price stability and the absence of price competition. This has not stemmed from the existence of a price leader or from price agreements but from a realization of the riskiness of price cutting on the one hand, and the need to maintain the level of demand on the other. Experience had shown the industry that price cuts were not profitable unless the demand for the particular product was elastic, and that if competitors retaliated they would all be worse off. The price changes that occurred suggest a considerable independence of action among producers and no form of price agreement.

In the 1930's the trade was largely in the hands of six major producers – Austin, Morris, Ford, Vauxhall, Standard, Rootes – and competition had eliminated many of the smaller firms or forced them out of the popular-car market into the more specialist class. There was little room for the exercise of monopoly powers: indeed, the market share of the leaders, Austin and Morris, was considerably reduced by the other four big producers. But the gap between the big six and the 'specialists' was widening. The bargaining advantages, technical economies, research facilities and retail network of the larger firms were decisive in pushing the others out of the popular market. The competitive process which brought this about was the frequent introduction of a new model at a competitive price. The smaller firms could not afford the expensive 'tooling' which new models involved. They did not have the scale of production to make frequent change an economic proposition. Maxcy & Silberston suggest that 'model-price' competition is the most active form of long-run competition in the industry before the Second World War, and changes in the market shares of the Big Six can best be explained in terms of successful models.

In this period between the two world wars there had been no rigid pattern in the market structure of the motor industry. Although a growth in the scale of production favoured the larger firms, Austin and Morris, which dominated the market at the beginning of the period, lost ground to those of their smaller rivals which were able to adopt mass production techniques. The fluctuating fortunes of the six biggest manufacturers show that there was genuine competition, and that what elements there were of monopoly power in the market did not save the Big Six downswings of fortune. Few of the independent specialist producers enhanced their position significantly in this period. Apart from missing out on the economies of scale enjoyed by the larger firms, they had none of their bargaining power. Many disappeared from the scene, while others sold out to the large firms. This was the typical merger of this period: between small and larger producer.

In the period since the Second World War other types of mergers

79

have occurred. The most important have been those between the large producers, operating similar processes, producing similar products – horizontal integration, and those between the large producers and firms supplying essential components – vertical integration. The mergers between Austin and Morris to form the British Motor Corporation in 1952, the merger between Ford and Briggs Motor Bodies in 1953, and that between Rootes and Singer Motors in 1955 are good examples of integration in the first half of this period. An attempt is made to show the effect of these mergers on market shares in the table below, but the absence of statistics for the war period reduces the value of the table.

			% share of market			
	Austin–Morris (B.M.C. in 1952)		Ford	Rootes	Standard	Vauxhall
1938	25·6	22·2	19·0	11·1	10·8	11·3
1939	26·9	24·3	14·7	10·9	12·8	10·4
1946	43·4		14·4	10·7	11·6	9·0
1950	39·4		19·2	13·5	11·1	9·0
1953	35·2		27·0	12·8	8·6	10·4
1955	39·0		26·5	11·5	9·5	8·5
1960	36·5		30·0	10·5	8·0	11·0

(From tables by J. Maxcy and A. Silberston, *The Motor Industry*.)

There was a considerable change in market conditions after the war as compared with those which had existed in the pre-war market. Before the war manufacturers had had to work hard to stimulate demand for their products. Models were changed frequently to attract new customers, and the long production runs which bring economies of scale were not common. After the war the market favoured the producers: they could not produce cars fast enough to meet the demand. Order books lengthened as shortages of materials and skilled labour remained acute. Rising costs could easily be passed on in rising prices, and producers strove to increase their output of cars knowing they could easily sell all that they could produce. The big producers were able to use their bargaining power to secure the essential supplies of materials which were one of the limiting factors in production. In this production race the small independent producers were hardest hit. They were at the mercy of suppliers and usually had to take their turn behind the Big Six when supplies were short. The stronger manufacturers took measures to safeguard their supplies particularly by adding to their body-building capacity.

Briggs merger with Ford in 1953 eased the supply situation for that producer.

There was little need for manufacturers to indulge in model price competition in such market conditions and thus changes in models were less frequent than before the war. This meant that production runs were longer and, with the large increase in the scale of production, the economies to the big manufacturer were considerable. Interchangeability of parts between models was becoming standard practice and this gave further cost benefits to the Big Five. The same engines were being used in a whole range of cars, and in this way the costly process of research, development and tooling up for each new model was kept as low as possible, and much longer engine production runs were achieved. B.M.C. had three basic engines for several models in the 1950's. Modifications could be made to the engine and to the car to enable the company to offer the public a significantly different model, without the costly disadvantages of a 'new' model. The policy of the Big Five has been to change models less frequently, but to offer variety on the basic model. Their main object in this policy has been to keep costs at a minimum for the reluctance of the manufacturers to compete through price meant that costs were the main factor determining profit margins.

Mass production was a big advantage and in this competition through efficiency, those who failed to increase their scale of production in step with the growth of the industry suffered severely through profit margins. Even in the expensive saloons and sports cars, the partial mass production of the big manufacturers gave them an advantage. One of the small firms to be hit by these trends were Singer Motors, which were acquired by Rootes in 1955. By 1956 only the Big Five were competing in the popular market.

There were various forms of competition in the trade. Although new models were less frequent than before the war, model changes still occurred more frequently than would have happened if the industry had been dominated by a single producer like Volkswagen. Even when they could sell all they could produce of any model they were reluctant to let their rivals completely dominate any given range in the market. Apart from competition through costs, and competition in each range, the Big Five strove to increase their sales by offering better services. The distribution of their products and retail salesmanship were also important if they were to make the most of a wide market. It was pressure from the dealers which persuaded the manufacturers to offer a wide range of models. In this way the dealer was able to meet the competition at every price range of his nearby rival. Maxcy and Silberston point out that 'although price elasticity of demand for vehicles in general is not very high, the cross elasticity of demand between vehicles of different makes is undoubtedly considerable'.

	1955	1960	1961	1962	1963	1964	1965
B.M.C.	39	36·5	38·5	37·5	38·5	37	37·2
Ford	26·5	30	32·5	29·5	31·5	28·5	33·3
Rootes	11·5	10·5	9·5	11·5	10·5	12·0	9·9
St/Trium.	9·5	8·0	6·5	6·0	6·5	6·5	6·8
Vauxhall	8·5	11·0	8·5	11·5	10·0	13·5	7·9
Others	5·0	4·0	4·5	3·5	3·0	3·0	4·9

During the decade after 1955 the process of integration continued and became even more significant. The trend whereby a growing proportion of the trade was concentrated in the hands of the Big Five was accelerated. Some of the mergers which have occurred since the war appear to have been defensive reactions on the part of manufacturers to maintain their position in the market. The Austin–Nuffield merger occurred when both had been losing ground. Ford acquired Briggs when supplies of materials were still short, and the merger between Rootes and Singer came when Rootes had slipped back in the production race and Singer were suffering from the small scale of their production. In the mergers of the 1955–65 period a similar influence can be found. Standard's arrangement with Mulliners in 1958 was part of a trend whereby car manufacturers integrated vertically with independent body-builders. B.M.C. had taken an important step towards integration when they acquired Fisher–Ludlow (who also supplied some of Standard's bodies) in 1953, just six months after the Ford–Briggs merger. The culmination of the trend was the acquisition of Pressed Steel by B.M.C. in 1965, which will be examined in more detail later.

The small firms had been aided in the past by the vertical disintegration and diversification which were characteristic of firms in the industry. These characteristics explain why no British firm could be said to be operating at its optimum, unlike firms in Germany (Volkswagen), Italy (Fiat) and France (Renault). In America, General Motors has several plants operating at optimum level and enjoying full economies of scale. It was the need to compete with these in firms the export markets which gave impetus to further mergers among manufacturers in Britain. Standard Triumph cleared the way for its merger with Leyland Motors in 1961, when it sold its tractor producing facilities to Massey–Ferguson in 1959. Leyland added to its holdings in 1962 when it acquired its chief rival in the heavy commercial vehicle field, A.C.V. This horizontal integration between two heavy vehicle producers enabled economies to be gained in this field. The struggle for further economies by the motor manufacturers explains their growing interest in the export trade. It provided an outlet for the extra units which had to be produced if the firms were to expand towards the optimum size. In 1966 of the 1·6 million cars produced over 600,000 were exported. B.M.C. exported some 40 per cent of its production to 163 countries. Of the smaller firms Jaguar and Rover seemed most aware of the need to expand to achieve economies. In 1960 Jaguar acquired Daimler from B.S.A., in 1961 Guy Motors, and in 1963 Coventry Climax. Rover merged with Alvis in 1965. Both Jaguar and Rover came to realize in 1965 that their only hope to remain in production was to merge with one of the Big Five. Jaguar joined B.M.H. and Rover joined Leyland Motors.

Diversification of product is a valuable way of spreading the risk of a fall in the demand in one market, and this must have been an important motive in the Leyland–Standard Triumph merger and the Jaguar–Guy Motors merger.

The great American motor manufacturers, General Motors, Ford, and Chrysler have been looking increasingly to Europe for further investment opportunities, as the American market seems to be approaching saturation point. General Motors have competed successfully in the British market through Vauxhall, and in the 1960's extended their range of models and built a new plant at Merseyside. In 1960 Ford of America were allowed to purchase the remaining share capital of Ford of Dagenham. The most recent expansion of American interest in the British Motor industry has been the acquisition by Chrysler of a majority holding in Rootes in 1965. The British Government agreed to this merger on the assurance that Chrysler would not take over control from the Rootes Board, and the Industrial Reorganization Corporation lent £3 million to assist in the development of production. The Government had considered and rejected the idea that Rootes should be taken over by the State, and no other British firms were interested in acquiring the company, so it was not considered necessary to refer the merger to the Monopolies Commission, which could have been required under the Monopolies and Mergers Act of 1965, governing any merger involving over £5 million.

The first merger to be examined under this act was that by which B.M.C., Jaguar Cars Ltd., and Pressed Steel Fisher amalgamated into British Motor Holdings in 1965-6. B.M.C.'s Chairman outlined the main arguments for the merger in a company statement. He said the merger is 'in line with the world trend towards larger and more comprehensive units'. 'The bigger units are better equipped to secure the economies of large-scale production.' To remain fully competitive in world markets B.M.C. had to follow the trend towards competition by a few large firms. (The Government has also emphasized the need for British manufacturers to co-operate in the overseas market.)

The more specific advantages outlined were the strengthened links with the supplying industries (Pressed Steel), the extended range of cars and commercial vehicles which would result from combination between firms which were complementary and not competitive (Jaguar), the wider market coverage, the improved facilities for distribution and service at home and abroad, and the stronger financial and commercial position of the new company.

Before the merger Pressed Steel had been the only remaining independent large producer of car bodies. It was responsible for about 40 per cent of the total output, and was the chief source of supply for Rootes Group as well as supplying B.M.C. and Standard/Triumph. The position was such that B.M.H. would have had a considerable bargaining advantage over Pressed Steel's other customers. The Monopolies Commission therefore secured an undertaking that Pressed Steel's present customers would continue to be served. The Pressed Steel Linwood Plant was sold to Rootes. The Commission allowed the merger because 'we think that there is some appreciable advantage in Pressed Steel being taken over by a British rather than a foreign company. If it had remained independent either B.M.C. or Rootes would have set up their own production of bodies and this would have meant a "wasteful duplication of national resources".'

The merger between B.M.H. and Leyland early in 1968 had many interesting features. It seems that the main driving force behind the merger was not so much B.M.H. with about one-third of the market, but Leyland with only one-tenth. The Government supplied further impetus through the Industrial Reorganization Corporation, with a loan of £25m to assist the rationalization of the two companies. The Board of Trade announced that there would be no objections to the merger to put before the Monopolies Commission.

British Leyland Motor Corporation is now the third largest motor manufacturing group outside the U.S., and the fifth largest of all companies in Britain. Only General Motors, Ford, Chrysler, Fiat and Volkswagen have a larger output of motor vehicles. It is better placed to meet the growing competition from these giants in the export markets, and from their subsidiaries in the home market. In 1967 the combined output of Leyland and BMH was more than 893 thousand out of a total for all producers of just under 2 million. In 1967–68 the 250,000 British Leyland workers produced £900m's worth of vehicles, £500m sold at home, and £400m overseas (£275m direct exports), the remainder produced in plant overseas. British Leyland produced 45 per cent of total vehicle production which topped the 2 million mark in spite of Government restrictions on home demand. But in the first quarter of 1969 sales by foreign manufacturers in the British market had almost reached 10 per cent.

| | Total for 1967 | | Total for 1968 | | Jan–March 1969 | |
	Cars '000	C.V.'s '000	Cars '000	C.V.'s '000	Cars '000	C.V.'s '000
B.M.C.	540	107	609	105⎤	117	17
Jaguar	22	3	24	3	6	24*
Total	562	110	633	108	—	—
Leyland	123	24	139	24	38	—
Rover	43	31	47	37	12	11
Total	166	55	189	61⎦	232	† 52
Ford	441	94	554	108	108	26
Rootes	181	29	189	27	52	8
Vauxhall	197	89	245	97	56	32

See Appendix 3.   † Total Br. Leyland.   * B.L. Truck and Bus Division.

A programme of rationalization began in 1968 designed to make the most of B.L.M.C.'s productive potential of 1,100,000, vehicles p.a.

The advantages likely to accrue from the merger are many, and B.L.M.C. will benefit from the general economies of scale which are opened up by the combined capital strength, and from the pooling of ideas on research and marketing, engineering and development. Although the productive units are largely complementary, there is a good deal of room for rationalization, particularly of engines and bodies. B.L.M.C. dealers will have an unrivalled range of models to deal in, while the firm will enjoy marketing economies from the combined outlets. With a capital strength of £400m, B.L.M.C. will be better able to weather the market fluctuations and product failures inevitable in the industry, and to meet the costs of new model development, as well as the intensive competition in world markets.

The main object of the mergers of recent years has been to produce an integrated firm operating at the optimum level for the given state of technical knowledge. The trends towards greater concentration and rationalization of models – bodies and engines have produced fewer firms and bigger firms but there seems to have been no abatement in the intensity of competition between these firms. The existence of agreements between members of the Motor Industry Research Association, the National Advisory Council for Motor Manufacturing Industries, and the Society of Motor Manufacturers and Traders, to co-operate on such matters as standardization and to exchange technical information, has had virtually no effect in limiting competition between firms. Collective Resale Price Maintenance does operate in the industry, and certain sectors of the Trade – tyres, electrical equipment – have been shown to be guilty of restraints on competition, but restrictive practices are absent from the market for motor vehicles. The existence of a group which controls more than one-third of the market has not resulted in the exercise of monopoly powers which are against the public interest.

B.L.M.C. make three comments on this study of their marketing environment:

1. B.L.M.C.'s apparent position of major strength, i.e. over 40 per cent of the domestic car market, is far removed from a monopoly position in as far as the Corporation is competing with General Motors, Ford U.S., and Chrysler through their U.K. subsidiaries – a totally different set of circumstances than if such subsidiaries were independent local producers.

2. In today's circumstances we agree that the essence of competition is least of all price and much more the achievement of total effective marketing of the product. Thus the competitive element is projected through substantial expenditure on advertising and sales promotion, on improving distribution effectiveness through business efficiency and standard accounting procedures and a thorough and detailed knowledge of the market. Competition is a matter of effective stocking, of matching vehicle availability to the seasonal movement in demand and of course, the proper concept of new model timing and model change. All these would take priority over general price cutting.

3. Profit is no longer a matter of making an independent unit sum of each vehicle produced, but results from continuous intensive study and implementation of the most economic forms of production relevant to scale: the American subsidiaries in the U.K. because of their transatlantic connections are at no disadvantage whatsoever in this connection.

SELECTED BIBLIOGRAPHY

Monopolies Commission Reports, 1954, Oxygen.

Monopolies Commission Reports, 1961, Tobacco.

Monopolies Commission Reports, 1966, B.M.C. – Pressed Steel.

P. Lesley Cook and Ruth Cohen, *Effects of Mergers*.

Phelps Brown, *Applied Economics*.

E. A. G. Robinson, *Monopoly*.

The Bow Group, *Monopolies and Mergers*.

Keesings Contemporary Archives.

J. K. Galbraith, Reith Lectures.

J. Maxcy and A. Silberston, *The Motor Industry*.

A. Silberston, *The Motor Industry 1955–64*.

Vol. 27 No. 3. Oxford University Institute of Economics & Statistics.

Journal of the Society of Motor Manufacturers and Traders.

APPENDIX 1

Resale Price Maintenance in the Tobacco Trade

The most serious challenge to the limitation on price competition resulting from the oligopolistic situation in the tobacco industry has been the
pressure on producers to end Resale Price Maintenance following the
passing of the Resale Prices Act in 1964 (see pp. 42–45). R.P.M. became
illegal for all goods except those filed for exemptions hearings in the
Restrictive Practices Courts by the manufacturers. The Tobacco manufacturers duly filed their application and withdrew only when, after the
confectioners lost their petition, the position became hopeless. Meanwhile, to delay the impact the manufacturers in their attempt to keep
some control over the retail prices of their product adopted the expedients
of "recommended prices" and refusal to supply retailers who ignored
these directives. A recent Monopolies Commission report has, with few
exceptions, condemned these practices.

The manufacturers defended r.p.m. by arguing that greater damage to
the public interest would result from its removal in that the number of
retail outlets and the standard of service would be reduced, while the
pressure of increased price competition in such a highly concentrated
industry would be towards mergers and even more concentration, so
that prices would as a result rise more in the long run. Moreover, they
argued that average profit margins in the industry were not excessive.

The experience of 1968 and 1969 suggests there is some force in these
arguments. Tobacconists have seen a perceptible proportion of their
trade transferred to the supermarkets (some 18 per cent of the sale of
cigarettes). But their total sales of all goods have increased by 8 per cent

on the £1,030m of 1966. The bargaining power of the big supermarket groups vis-à-vis the manufacturers has increased and price cutting is gaining momentum. The Co-ops, Woolworths, and off-licences followed the supermarkets, and for popular brands cuts of 3d on a packet of 20 usually costing 4s 10d were common. A big supermarket threatened to begin producing its own brand of cigarette.

Indirect price competition has also been boosted, and a spate of coupons, gifts and advertising has assailed the consumer. Meanwhile merger discussions have gone ahead, but chiefly with American firms wanting to enter the market, and tobacco manufacturers, particularly Imperial, Gallaher and British American, have sought ways of diversifying their activities. However, in 1968 Imperial still depended for 88 per cent of their trading profits (£41m) on tobacco sales, and with the number of cigarettes and the quantity of tobacco used showing no tendency to diminish the stormy conditions resulting from the abolition of r.p.m. seem to have been successfully ridden out. Indeed with profits of £47·5m (20 per cent up on 1967) on sales of £1,200m, even the deterrent of tax impositions and the rising cost of non-Rhodesian leaf will cause no serious concern.

APPENDIX 2

Relative Strength[1] of Tobacco Companies in Britain 1968–69
[taken from 'The Times' 500]

	British[2] American	Imperial	Gallaher	Carreras	Godfrey Phillips	Rothmans
Rank among largest British firms	5th	6th	46th	107th	341st	398th
Capital Employed	£495m	£447m	£116m	£48m	£12m	£10m
Profit 1968–69	£105m	£50m	£16m	£6·2m	£2·7m	£2·2m
Profit 1967–68	£103m	£48m	£16·5m	£6·0m	£2·2m	£2·0m
Rank among profit British earners	4th	6th				
Sales	£1,051m	£945m	£392m	£42m		
Rank among sellers	3rd	5th				
Employees	88,000	47,500	14,400		2,713	

[1] Business not confined to sales of cigarettes and tobacco.
[2] British America has no tobacco sales in U.K.

INDEX